BYACHAD

Byachad

Synagogue Board Development

Robert Leventhal

THE
ALBAN
INSTITUTE

Herndon, Virginia
www.alban.org

The Alban Institute
2121 Cooperative Way, Ste. 100
Herndon, VA 20171

ISBN 978-1-56699-352-4

Revised second printing.

CONTENTS

ACKNOWLEDGEMENTS

Byachad emerged from a series of community-wide workshops sponsored by the UJA-Federation of New York in 2005 and 2006. These three workshops for synagogue leaders dealt with the Leadership Plan, the Delegation Plan, and the Accountability Plan and included ideas from the nonprofit world, the business world and the congregational world to help leaders imagine a new approach to board leadership. Participants described some of the challenges they faced trying to bring these ideas to their boards. This inspired us to develop workshops that could be done with the whole board of a single congregation—hence the *Byachad* workbook. Experience taught us that "it takes a community to change a practice." UJA-Federation of New York helped us recruit the initial congregations and supported them on their leadership-development journey.

I would like to thank Erika Witover, chair of the Synagogue Task Force of the Commission on Jewish Identity and Renewal and Dru Greenwood, Director of Synagogue Renewal for their encouragement and support in bringing this project to fruition. I would also like to thank Rabbi Deborah Joselow and Dr. Alisa Rubin Kurshan for their vision of a vibrant Jewish future informed by knowledgeable, inspired, and caring Jewish leaders.

Introduction

Welcome to *Byachad: Synagogue Board Development*. One of the signs of a vital congregation is its leadership. Prospective leaders and members may look at our building, programs, and brochures, but they will also take the measure of our leadership. Do our leaders seem to take joy in Jewish living? Does Judaism make our leaders' board governance something special—something of which prospective leaders and members may want to be a part?

When I meet with congregations, the most common question I hear is "How do we develop new leaders?" A close second is "How do we engage more of our members?" Dr. Amy Sales, reflecting on her survey of congregations in Westchester County, New York, asserts that "the absence of a systematic approach to congregant development has far-reaching consequences." Synagogue Board Development is an attempt to build board consensus about critical governance functions and to create a systematic plan to motivate and support leaders in developing new practices.

Not all of your board members may feel as if they are born leaders, but according to Dr. Ronald Heifetz, author of *Leadership without Easy Answers*, most can develop leadership skills by doing leadership tasks. In our tradition our rituals and observances help us learn by doing. We may not be comfortable with strategic theory, but we can learn to ask strategic questions. Dr. Arnold Eisen argues in *Taking Hold of Torah* that the genius of Leviticus is that it provides rituals we can do. The Israelites might not have understood all of the Jewish theology, but they could experience the holy through ritual practices. In *Byachad* I have focused on a few board rituals that I feel are particularly supportive of new leadership work.

Board teamwork should be designed to build more enduring relationships among lay leaders and between leaders and the staff. Teams need to focus on shared congregational goals so that leaders can provide the right direction, make the right assignments, and provide the right feedback. We need to encourage leaders to review their maps and take a fresh look at their leadership.

Corporate learning experts John Seely Brown and Estee Solomon Gray write in their introduction to *Creating a Learning Culture* that the twenty-first century requires that leaders have a collaborative mind and become a leadership team by doing leadership work together. "It takes a community to change a practice," they say.[1] To build capacity, we have to learn to read those maps together.

> IN BYACHAD I HAVE FOCUSED ON A FEW BOARD RITUALS THAT I FEEL ARE PARTICULARLY SUPPORTIVE OF NEW LEADERSHIP WORK.

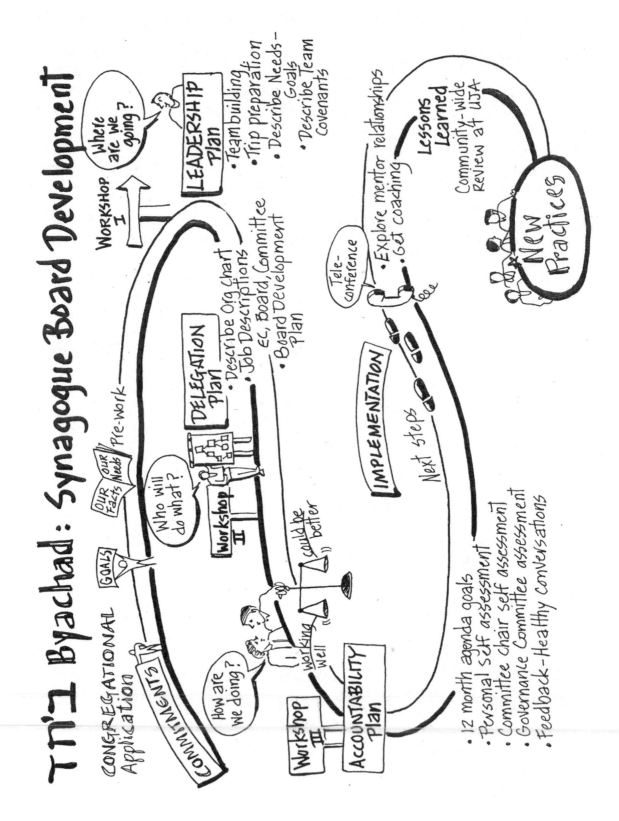

1

Byachad

It Takes a Community to Change a Practice

The board is going to change by what it learns and what it does. Leaders should consider some of the elements of their learning culture. What attitudes are giving energy to the leadership's learning? What helps them step forward to learn more about each other, the community, their Jewish mission, and their work together? What gets in the way?

We Learn by Doing Together

The Israelites replied to God at Sinai, "Na-aseh v'nishma"—"We will do and we will obey" (Exod. 24:7). Some have translated this "We will do and we will understand." According to Talmudic legend (Eitz Hayim, p. 478), the angels were so moved by this courage that they put a crown on each Israelite's head. We are asking leaders to step forward into *Byachad* before they fully understand the benefits of this kind of leadership development. Like the midrash of Nacshon at the Red Sea, SBD participants will have to commit first—they will have to get their feet wet. That takes courage! As these ideas emerge and become resonant in a deeper, richer way, leaders will be able to tell new stories about their leadership team and their evolving team practices.

The Jewish world is full of helpful practices. There are denominational guides, books on congregational practices, articles, and training models. All of these tools were grown and developed in a specific context. If we are to learn from them, we must plant the ideas they give us *in our community*. The board must choose what seeds to nurture, protect, and celebrate.

The Leadership Seder

Synagogue Board Development encourages new rituals and practices. I coined the term "leadership seder" because I think that it is important to have some step-by-step process to learn new behaviors. The word *seder* means order. The Passover seder works to ensure that the most important lessons of the Jewish people are learned by all of the family's members. The seder leaders are challenged to find effective ways to communicate with all different kinds of learners. This is captured in the texts relating to the four sons. The seder appeals to all kinds of learners with all kinds of motivations. We start Byachad by reviewing each participant's profile. We want to understand who is at our table.

The board table can become set in its ways. During the Passover seder, we make sure that people realize this night is not like every other. They hold their body in a new posture (recline on pillows). Our *Byachad* table is set to encourage members to get to know each other. It is set to explore our assumptions about our relationships. The facilitator—like an effective seder leader—works to get everyone involved. All have a seat at the table. All have a part. All who are hungry for leadership are invited.

In chapter 2, "Developing Leadership Gifts," in my new book, *Kadima,* I state that not everyone may feel as if he or she is born a leader, but most can learn to do leadership work. One leader may not be able to train another to be a leader, but together they can learn synagogue leadership at the leadership seder table as a "community of practice."

Byachad means "together." The Synagogue Board Development training process will help the president, the executive committee, the board, and other committees better understand how to work effectively together. When these groups pull in different directions, the organization suffers from a lack of alignment. When your tires are not aligned, they wear out and the ride gets bumpy. Likewise, poor alignment wears out teams and creates waste. Shared meaning and shared covenants create new energy. Synagogue board training was inspired by the work of Mark Light, *The Strategic Board*. It involves three board training sessions focusing on the *leadership plan*, the *delegation plan*, and the *accountability plan*.

Leadership Plan: Who Are We? What Is Our Purpose?

The leadership plan asks, "Who are we?" What are the values and guiding principles that should shape our leadership work? Do we believe in participation, collaboration, courage, and accountability? If so, how might these things be reflected in our work? Research shows that most synagogue members are not used to reflecting on how Jewish values or traditions should guide important decisions. Many rabbis, while knowledgeable about the tradition, have not found a forum to convene these conversations. Before they gather consumer data about their members' wants and needs, rabbis look to core Jewish values and practices. With a four-thousand-year-old tradition, leaders do not need to create a whole new garment. While leaders need to be steady in purpose (God, Torah, and Israel), they need to be flexible in strategy (How might this board work to fulfill this mission today, to better weave the tradition into our current practice?).

Each leadership team, like the biblical kings of old, must take a fresh look at the tradition and come to grips with it—to write their own Torah. "And it shall be, when he sits on the throne of kingship, that he shall write for himself a copy of the teachings in a book before the levitical priests. And it shall be with him and he shall read in it all the days of his life, so that he may learn to fear the Lord his God, to keep all of the words of his teaching and these statutes" (Deut. 17:18-19).

The leadership plan encourages leaders to let go of the minutia—potholes in the parking lot and the newsletter that is going out late—and, instead, to get up in the balcony where they can see the whole congregation, its context (environment and culture), and the tradition. One tool that will help them gain a perspective is the Congregational Needs Assessment (see appendix A).

Synagogue Leadership Literacy: Briefing Books

To be an effective leader, you must have a basic understanding of Jewish tradition. Immersing yourself in Jewish learning helps you step out of the day-to-day modern American culture and take a fresh look at how Judaism looks at life, living, and leading. You may want to design an adult education curriculum about leadership topics, such as practices, ethics, history, philosophy and theology, and worship. I would be happy to brainstorm with your team about the various approaches and resources (Synagogue 3000 is an excellent one) that might help them address this material.

Leaders are also challenged to be literate about the synagogue environment and the synagogue organization. They need to understand key trends, factors, and forces and have a grasp on their demographics, attendance, membership, financial situation, and so on. They need to attain a "lay of the land." "See what the land is . . . and whether the land is rich or poor" (Num. 13:18-20).

I will help the board create a congregational profile board briefing book of the most important facts that leaders need to know about trends, current programs, demographics, and finances. The book will also include the board's needs assessment.

Goals

Leaders need to know the lay of the land as well as a sense of where their path leads. They need to ask the strategic question, "Where should we be going now?" The leadership plan emphasizes goal conversations because they help a diverse set of leaders come together and be aligned. Goals are a critical requirement for teamwork and communications. How can we empower professional and volunteer leaders to do their work without goals? I like to start with broad long-term goals, because when leaders go into the future, they are more open to new approaches.

DELEGATION PLAN

Leaders often complain that a handful of people do most of the work. They may struggle to attract volunteers, but written goals make it easier for them to recruit people to leadership positions. Written job descriptions and well-defined policies and procedures have a direct impact on the leadership's capacity to fulfill their leadership

plan—to realize their Jewish mission. And when leaders hold themselves accountable for their goals, they gain the respect of leadership prospects. Prospects appreciate the authenticity (they are who they say) and integrity (they consistently strive to live their values) of such leaders.

Many potential leaders have been turned off by their experiences with poorly conceived and led projects. In one study 40 percent of the respondents said the reason they did not volunteer was because they already had and had been disappointed by the experience. Leaders need to hold themselves accountable to organize their committees and projects to use the gifts of their members most efficiently. The challenges of completing assignments in a timely and effective manner can be quite humbling. The development of humility (a core Jewish value) helps leaders become more empathetic about the challenges of professional and volunteer staff.

ACCOUNTABILITY PLAN

An accountability plan? I hear skeptics saying, "Yet another plan?" It's hard enough to get people to volunteer without holding them accountable. Yes, it's a challenge, but the research on the best nonprofits suggests they are doing just that. Just as our members face increasing accountability at work and set high expectations for their children, they should be expected to meet the standards set for their volunteer positions.

Likewise, if you have done the hard work of developing goals for your leadership and delegation plan, it is incumbent on your leadership to assess how you did. You hold yourself accountable in all other aspects of life, so why would you expect less from the shul? Start with the positive. List your committees on your Web page. Invite people to e-mail suggestions or to volunteer. Look for initiatives you can praise!

Accountable to Participate

We are committed to design workshops that are a mix of brainstorming, small group work, presentations, and Q&A and will always include a follow-up assignment. You may not understand all of the reasons for the processes, but you will be expected to participate fully. You are not expected to understand all of the theory, but you will be held accountable to do the leadership work. Accountability begins with shared values and goals and gains momentum when the executive committee provides leadership for chartering and supporting committees. It becomes critical when the board develops a twelve-month agenda to showcase key projects and to track the key initiatives. If they will a new agenda, it is no dream.

Workshop	Leadership Work	Outcome
1	Needs assessment—priorities, goals	Board expectations
2	Job descriptions (EC, BD) Board self-assesement	Board improvement plan Operating covenants
3	Individual leader self-assessment Committee chair self-assessment Board meeting progress check	Twelve-month agenda Communications plan

Implementing and developing these three plans sounds like a lot of work. Synagogue Board Development can work only if the participants are working on their assignments (e.g., reading, drafting agreements) between sessions. In the pages that follow, we offer you new tools, but leaders will need to take the time to practice with them.

WORKSHOP TOPICS

Workshop 1
Leadership Plan (Sunday Retreat)

MY LEADERSHIP

- Explore the Jewish experiences that have shaped your view of leadership.
- Explore what gives meaning to your volunteer work so that you can better recruit board prospects.

OUR LEADERSHIP

- Review the need assessment key issues
- Review the Alban Board Self-Assessment. Explore what is working well and what could be improved.
- Review how board process is helping you address congregational and board goals.

DESIRED OUTCOMES

- Develop Behavioral Covenants (agreements) for board members.
- Develop some strategies for a twelve-month board agenda.
- Begin process of developing SMART goals.

Workshop 2
Delegation Plan

MY ROLE

Review my role as an individual board member.
Reflect on my expectations and my level of commitment.

- Define the roles of the executive committee, the board, and the committee. Develop a job description for each.
- Review lay staff roles and communications. Review the synagogue's organizational structure.
- Explore helpful operating covenants for working together in this structure.
- Explore a timed agenda and ways to prioritize decisions.

DESIRED OUTCOMES

- Develop a Board Meeting Improvement Plan.
- Create SMART goals that provide clear direction and accountability to individuals and working groups.
- Create job descriptions for the executive committee, boards, and committees.

Workshop 3
Accountability Plan

MY ACCOUNTABILITY

- Explore how I can give and receive helpful feedback.

OUR ACCOUNTABILITY

- Develop a process to get feedback after every meeting-process check.
- The EC learns to track SMART goals throughout the year.
- Develop a self-assessment for all chairpersons.

DESIRED OUTCOMES

- Develop a trustee's or governance committee to review the board's progress.
- Develop a process to give feedback to chairs and use information to better design committees (charter, staff, etc.)
- Develop a communications plan to help communicate values, goals, and progress to the congregation.

Byachad Process Step	Description	Assignment after Workshop	Possible Dates
Teleconference with leaders	Review assignments to be performed. Review overall process	Get membership profiles for all participants. Create SBD congregational profile board briefing book. Do SBD needs assessment.	
Workshop 1: Leadership Plan	Do team building. Review needs assessment. Create SMART goals. Explore team behavioral covenants.	Refine SBD goal statements. Refine SBD behavioral covenants.	
Coaching call	Review assignments.	Prepare for Workshop 2.	
Workshop 2: Delegation Plan	Review job descriptions for EC, board, and committees. Review organizational chart.	Refine job descriptions and organizational chart.	
Coaching call	Review assignments.	Prepare for Workshop 3.	
Workshop 3: Accountability Plan	Review healthy congregational feedback. Develop 12-month agenda. Create governance team to get feedback on process.	Prepare 12-month agenda. Develop operating covenants for board meeting.	
Coaching call	Review progress. Prepare for community debrief.	Leaders prepare presentations.	
Sharing Byachad: community debriefing and celebration	Share stories with the congregation and celebrate work accomplished.	Continue to learn and grow.	

2

WORKSHOP 1

LEADERSHIP PLAN

WHY DO WE NEED A LEADERSHIP PLAN?

Synagogue leaders are responsible to plan for the future. We need to look at our environment and make some assumptions about the future. Leaders need to encourage foresight. In ancient days people often slept on their roofs, and parapets (short protective walls) surrounded the edges to keep them from falling off. A parapet was thus a symbol of a person's commitment to be responsible for the safety of those around them—to anticipate a whole range of hazards.

We are also taught not to harness the stronger ox with the weaker ass. The ox would overwhelm the ass, and the cart would not move smoothly. Again, we are to anticipate problems. If different parts of the leadership pull in different directions, the effort will be hurt. We will work to create a more coordinated team effort. We will review our goals and reflect on our board practices. Do our practices serve our mission and goals? Are they harnessed—aligned? Just as our ancestors looked around their environment and tried to identify hazards, so leaders must develop programs to ensure the viability of the congregation. As congregations grow and change, they need to plan their transitions. They prepare for transitions today by "sow-

ing" good practices so that the congregation can reap tomorrow.

To Provide an Honest Assessment

The most admired leadership quality, according to management scholars Barry Posner and James Kouzes, is to provide an honest assessment of the threats and opportunities in our environment. Our biblical ancestors had an agricultural tradition. They had to understand the changes in the seasons to survive. We believe a forward-looking and self-confident style has a powerful impact on followers. Kouzes and Posner note that the characteristic of being "positive and forward looking" is the second most admired leadership trait (after honesty). Leaders must overcome the negativity, anxiety, and fear that haunt so many communities. Like Joshua, they need to be realistic about the challenges ahead (i.e., conquest of the land) but tell a forward-looking story about God's mission.

LEADERS MUST PROVIDE AN HONEST ASSESSMENT AND A POSITIVE, FORWARD-LOOKING STORY.

To Help Leaders Be Positive and Forward Looking

I do a variety of brainstorming exercises with boards. I asked one group to tell me about the synagogue community. Almost all of the comments were about weaknesses and problems. The rabbi observed this and asked, "Why do any of you belong here?" In focusing on only the negatives, this group had lost focus of the "sweet fruits" of congregational life—High Holidays, life-cycle events, relationships, dedicated teachers, etc. It is essential that leaders balance what works with what needs to be improved. If a goal is too modest, it creates no energy. If it is too unrealistic, people may lose hope.

Numerous significant factors affect the nature of synagogue leadership. To in-crease effectiveness, synagogue leaders must learn to manage the synagogue environment, the synagogue context, and the synagogue organization.

Understanding the Synagogue Environment— Situation Analysis

Synagogue leaders often say to me, "It's just a shul. How complex can it be?" From a business perspective, these are clearly small businesses, but they are complex to manage.

In business we create a "situation analysis" to look at some of the forces that are creating threats or opportunities for our organization.

> REGARDLESS OF WHETHER A TREND IS POSITIVE OR NEGATIVE ("RICH OR POOR"), IT NEEDS TO BE UNDERSTOOD AND MANAGED.

Trends and Forces

If business leaders can come to some agreement about the forces that are impacting their organization, they can move forward to productively debate the implications of these forces. If you can't even convene a conversation on the trends and forces, how can you get to the more nuanced debate about the implications of them? We suggest you consider the trends and forces impacting your community. Are these of high, medium, or low significance?

Regardless of whether a trend is positive or negative ("rich or poor"), it needs to be understood and managed. Even assets like the Internet create challenges: How do we use this tool? How do we leverage it? How do we avoid some of the negative side effects associated with it—its impersonality and the risks of intemperate e-mail, for instance. In times of change, managing the environment takes work.

	Implications/Impact		
Examples: Trends-Forces		High	Medium	Low
Mobility			
Secularism			
High cost of Jewish living (home, schools, camps, congregations)			
Husband and wife working			
More interest in spirituality			
Internet increase communications			
More Jewish educational resources			

In the twenty-first century we have to take a fresh look at trends in volunteerism. In the old volunteer paradigm, people worked on a small project or event; they were later encouraged by veterans to be on a committee and ultimately on the board. This could take a period of years. Many talented leaders with substantial work or volunteer experience in other organizations are capable of going right to the board. They may not have the need or the patience to work their way up. There need to be opportunities for hands-on work and more strategic work.

When new leaders arrive, will we be ready? In a Brandeis study, "The Congregations of Westchester," not one congregation had a majority of respondents that agreed that their congregation was good at taking advantage of the talents and interests of members. Few agreed that the right leadership opportunities were being made available. Most members are not showing up, and when they do, they are not always effectively welcomed.

Leaders need to be able to step forward and challenge these trends. Ian Evison, formerly the director of research at the Alban Institute, writes about Jonah: "God's beef with the prophet Jonah did not lie with Jonah's general trend analysis. God rather agreed with Jonah that Nineveh was trending toward wickedness. God's beef with Jonah was that his understanding of the trend led him to go with what seemed like the obvious conclusion regarding what he ought to do—find a good ship out of town. His correct trend analysis led him to a failure of vision and nerve."

SWOT Analysis with a Forward-Looking Lens

Leaders need to develop some shared understanding about the synagogue environment and organization without jumping on the first boat away from Nineveh. Most of us are familiar with a SWOT analysis, a strategic planning tool that measures current internal characteristics—the strengths and weaknesses of an organization—and also looks at the external environment in terms of opportunities and threats. I encourage you to look at some of the hard facts in your environment. As you step forward, I encourage you to focus on how you can leverage your strengths to address future opportunities. By staying relatively more focused on the positive, you can avoid jumping on that first boat out of town.

ENGAGING THE OPPORTUNITIES IN OUR CONTEXT

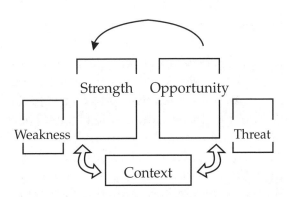

UNDERSTANDING THE SYNAGOGUE ORGANIZATION: HOW DO WE DO SHUL HERE?

Synagogue organizations present challenges to leaders trying to create cohesive communities in a world of change. According to Dr. Susan Shevitz, in *Congregation of Learners*, synagogues are distinguished by five characteristics: voluntary, pluralistic, loosely coupled, nonrational, and weak technology. The following are my reflections on these characteristics.

Voluntary

Volunteers come in and out of the organization. They are interested in some issues and not others. They may have a period of high energy and then fade when competing interests capture their attention. Understanding and managing volunteers is one of the central challenges of the synagogue leadership agenda. Leaders take into consideration that they are dealing with volunteers in a time of greatly diminished volunteer time. Authority in a voluntary environment is diffuse, writes Collins. There is not enough concentrated authority to ensure executive leadership. Nonprofit leaders cannot coerce action or pay incentives for performance.

Pluralistic

Congregations have a range of members with diverse needs. Unlike some businesses that can specialize, most congregations have to serve a broad constituency. They are not able to fully segment their programs and focus on a just a few profitable niches. They have a blueprint for community that comes from Torah, not from a business plan. Congregational leaders must find a way to hear the voice of families with preschool children as well as empty nesters. They need to anticipate the needs of both singles and seniors. Most synagogue leaders appreciate that they need to consider the needs of the whole community—*klal Yisrael*. A collaborative board is more likely to attend to the diverse needs of the congregation. A board should be big enough to handle the diversity of the congregation but small enough to work together effectively.

I was conducting a visioning workshop with a large, historic, multigenerational congregation. The older, more long-standing members were frustrated. They felt there had been too many changes in the congregation. At first they complained that new members were trying to "water down Conservative Judaism." This charge created conflict because it devalued the ideas of some newer members. As the process developed, the older members became more explicit about their concerns.

They were upset that their tunes had been changed by the cantor. Others were concerned that their High Holiday seats had been changed. Others were uncomfortable with some of the new approaches of the board. When they were asked to express all of these feelings as values, they argued that the congregation should "honor the synagogue's traditions." This was no longer a debate about who was a Conservative Jew. It was now developing into the issue of how to manage the rate of change.

I then asked them about the notes from the first workshop when the planning group had agreed that they needed to attract new members. The older members had all agreed this was a top priority. Membership had been declining. I asked if new members would want to come into a culture and agree not to change anything. The older members all laughed. They saw the absurdity of trying to hold on so tightly. In fact, all the tables of stakeholders saw they would have to find ways to honor existing stakeholders while making psychic space for new members if they were to grow in numbers or in creativity.

Loosely Coupled

Congregants may connect to some individuals and not to others. They may identify with some elements of the congregation's mission and not others. Synagogue observers have noted that many members have a "consumer orientation" rather than a membership orientation. Consumers are "loosely coupled" and focused on the service they are trying to procure, such as a bar mitzvah for a child. They may be connected to a certain program or may enjoy some social events. They do not see the holistic mission of the congregation and all of the diverse voices that make up the community.

Creativity comes from the interaction of the core with somewhat active members who have insights into the needs of seekers-prospects.

Nonrational

Scholars note that in business organizations there is a great deal of irrationality. Managers bring complex emotions to their work. Today business leaders speak of organizations as "swamps," where the footing is unstable and the visibility blocked, metaphorically speaking, by "heavy foliage and mist." If businesses are sometimes swamps, what are congregational environments like?

In business organizations, at least people share professional training as engineers, accountants, marketers, and lawyers. In contrast, synagogue leadership has a wide array of talents, experiences, and beliefs. Volunteers come with strong attachments, memories, beliefs, and positions. Many of these feelings lie below the surface and are not known to their congregational teammates. These emotions can come forward unexpectedly and without warning.

STORY: THE ANXIOUS AGENDA

A synagogue leader shared his dread over certain issues with his wife at the dinner table on the evening before a leadership meeting. Issue three was on the agenda tonight. It was going to be hot. He had heard the buzz about this topic for months, and now it was coming to the board. "I'll be home late tonight, dear," he said as he went out the door. When the board arrived at the meeting, issue three sailed through with only modest discussion. It turned out that issue four, the religious school field trip, was the hot one. How could this be? Why was an experienced board member fooled?

Unbeknownst to our board leader, issue four was an important personal issue to a few members. They remembered the poorly planned school field trip three years earlier. Their children had been on a bus that arrived late, and not enough box lunches had been prepared for the children. They forgot about lay staff boundaries and did not give the rabbi time to consult with the educator, even though she had the logistical details that would put their concerns to rest. They forgot the board's agenda and its priorities, even though other issues clearly were of greater weight to the vast majority of the board, and they wanted to thrash out their concerns in the middle of the meeting. Issue four turned out to be hot. Who would have guessed?

Weak Information

Good organizational leaders are reflective and learn from their mistakes. They grow by documenting the lessons they learn. Unfortunately, most congregations keep very poor records of committee and task forces. They invest little in orienting new team members so that prior learning can be transmitted.

STORY: FILE ON A HOLIDAY

When I do Synagogue Visioning and Planning I have several precontracting discussions about the process. One task is to identify the kind of data we need and to determine what is available. As I begin to go down my checklist, the other party often goes silent. I have to check to see if he or she is still on the line. I sense some anxiety about the depth and accessibility of the congregation's data.

In one instance, I tried to offer a simple confidence-building request. I asked, "Can I get a copy of the minutes of the education committee?" My planning partner then answered, "I will check, but I think she went to Boca." *Went to Boca?* I wondered. *How can the education committee's records have gone to Boca?*

The answer is that, as in so many congregations, there are few central files for many committees. They are the special preserve of individuals. The process is highly informal. Some recording secretaries take good minutes. Some hold on to them. Few ensure they are maintained or transferred to new leadership groups. Maintaining information about decisions and debriefing them is a core competency that allows leaders to "move up the learning curve"—to get smarter.

Preserving the legal debates between scholars was an extremely serious part of Jewish learning. We hear of this rabbi and that rabbi's views. Even the minority views that did not prevail were maintained (*Eduyot*). Despite this deep historic concern for honoring the past work of others, most

synagogue leaders have very inconsistent and sketchy records. What few are available may have headed south to Boca.

Dedicated Core of Leaders

After reviewing Shevitz's organizational characteristics, I decided to add one more. I often see a dedicated core leadership. While more than 80 percent of the congregation may not be consistently engaged with the congregation, there is a core group of leaders who are described by themselves and others as dedicated. The Westchester congregation study found that 5 percent were "greatly active" and another 14 percent were "very active." This study thus saw a core group of 19 percent. Most congregations concur with this assessment. These are the people you can count on to see in service at least twice a month. They come to major events. They are working with some committee or group each year.

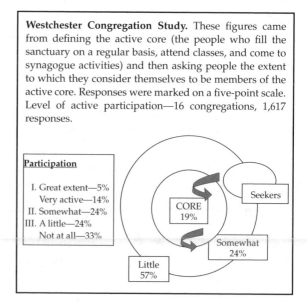

Westchester Congregation Study. These figures came from defining the active core (the people who fill the sanctuary on a regular basis, attend classes, and come to synagogue activities) and then asking people the extent to which they consider themselves to be members of the active core. Responses were marked on a five-point scale. Level of active participation—16 congregations, 1,617 responses.

Participation

I. Great extent—5%
   Very active—14%
II. Somewhat—24%
III. A little—24%
    Not at all—33%

CORE 19%

Seekers

Somewhat 24%

Little 57%

Overcoming Internal Focus

One of the challenges of synagogue life is to help the inner circle (19 percent) find ways for the less engaged to connect and be more active. It is not uncommon for the very active to spend years overfunctioning "to keep the synagogue running." As they do this they often develop a style of doing business and become set in their ways. When new ideas are presented, they may say, "That won't work; we've tried it before."

Some dominant leaders may interrupt conversations and redirect the discussion to their approach. Reactive core leaders may resist innovation. Congregational creativity occurs when there is an interaction between core leaders and motivated, gifted leaders who come from the periphery, that is, from those who are somewhat involved and who have insights into the needs of seekers, or prospects.

Synagogue Board Development addresses the challenge of recruiting and orienting new leaders and helping old leaders move in and out of core roles (boards, committees). It also has the responsibility of making sure that real leadership opportunities are available to them. This means ensuring that there are term limits for current members, that board meetings are designed to welcome new members (e.g., through a summer picnic), and that *derech eretz* can be maintained to protect new ideas and new leaders. Most groups can't succeed just by working harder with old approaches—they need new tools and new people to change direction.

STRATEGIES THAT ADDRESS THE SPECIAL CHALLENGES OF THE SYNAGOGUE ORGANIZATION

Characteristics	Strategy
Voluntary	Must motivate and train
Pluralistic	Need a diverse group of leaders
Loosely Coupled	Provide short-term projects—catch them when they are in the building, at events
Nonrational	Accept this factor—provide more time to work through issues as you build common ground
Weak Information	Learn to build written resources—goals, visions, committee charters, narrative notes
Dedicated Core Leaders	Acknowledge their past service; encourage them to set the leadership seder tables in ways that make room for more family members and different types of Jews.

Question

When you think of the unique challenges of the synagogue organization, what kinds of leadership approaches are helpful?

CONGREGATIONAL LEADERSHIP QUALITIES

Is your board talking about your congregational environment? Are you developing strategies to address the unique challenges of your synagogue organization? In a 2005 study of 14,301 congregations, the Hartford Institute looked at how certain leadership practices impacted growth.

The fact is, leadership requires a commitment and intentional planning. Leaders have to commit to learn their craft. "The nut tree is smooth. Anyone who would climb to its top without considering how to do it is sure to fall, thus taking his punishment from the trees. So too, he who would exercise authority over a community in Israel without considering how to do it is sure to fall and take his punishment from the hands of the community" (Song of Songs *Rabbah* 6:11).

To guide a community, leaders must learn new ideas and create a practice field to try out new approaches. Not everyone was born a leader but we believe that leaders can grow by doing leadership work. Hal Lewis reminds us that the word for a leader is *man-*

Leadership	Research Findings	Research Findings	What Boards Can Do
Purpose-driven congregations grow.	Strongly disagree or unsure: 16%, growing	Strongly agree: 43%, growing	Develop a vision of what the impact of the synagogue should be.
Spiritually vital congregations grow.	Strongly disagree or unsure: 14%, growing	Strongly agree: 45%, growing	Help people move from consumers to leaders and disciples. Increse the energy of the team.
Congregation is *willing to change* to meet new challenges.	Strongly disagree or unsure: 15%, growing	Strongly agree: 45%, growing	Create a practice field for leaders to experiment, grow, and change.
Conflict in congregation in two years	Nonconflict: 13%, declining	Major conflict: 42%, declining	Clarify expectations about roles, responsibilities, behavior, and practices. Create healthy conversations.

C. Kirk Hadaway, *Facts on Growth—Faith Communities*, Hartford Institute for Research, 2006.

According to the Facts on Growth table above, congregations that can define their purpose and goals and create spiritual energy (discipleship) and are willing to try new things are thriving! Unfortunately, most congregational leadership groups are overly managerial and tactical—not leadership focused.

hig, which derives from the three-letter root *nun-hey-gimel* meaning "behavior." It comes from the same root as *minhag*, which means "practice."

We need to change our practice of recruitment. C. Jeff Woods writes in *Congregational Megatrends* that we have entered a time when core leaders need to look beyond official leaders (current board and core groups) to "gifted leaders," those who have passion and talents that may not have been captured by the synagogue. Recruiters need to throw out a broader net and reach out to new waters.

Defining congregational purpose and the roles and responsibilities of leaders reduces conflict and builds teamwork and helps congregations grow.

Managing the Leadership Pole

Alban uses an instrument called the Congregational Systems Inventory (CSI), developed by George Parsons and Speed Leas, to measure the leadership styles of congregations. Leadership is one of the seven dimensions studied. The "managerial pole" is on one end of the continuum. It is practical and tactical. On the other end is the "transformational pole." It is visionary and strategic.

Leadership

Managerial									Transformational
1	2	3	4	5	6	7	8	9	10

Leas believes that both styles are important. If a leader thinks only about mission and purposes, he or she may fail to balance the budget or pay the utility bill. Most boards are managerial. They score about 2. Smaller congregations tend to be more managerial—they have few staff and many hands—on tasks. In Jewish terms, we need to balance the tension between *eretz* (the practical and earthly) and *shemayim* (the spiritual and visionary). Without a vision,

the people perish. If we are focused only on the utility bills, we may not pay enough attention to why we are maintaining the building (growth characteristics—purpose driven, spiritual, open-curious). What are we trying to achieve? Who are we trying to invite?

Leas has argued that management and leadership are polarities. They are tensions to be managed, not problems to be solved. If we allow our leadership to get too far to one side of the continuum, it is harder to stay in touch with the imperatives of the other pole. In practical terms, when we go too far on the managerial pole, we forget what it's like to dream as an 8 to 10. When someone comes with an idea from the visionary or experimental realm, we may not see the gift he or she brings. Leaders are not consciously trying to be unwelcoming—they simply can't hear the message from the other pole.

I ask leadership groups to cross their arms. *Hard!* Then I ask them to cross them the other way. It feels funny, doesn't it? We have a lot of muscle memory about how to sit in board meetings. Some are extroverted and lean forward. Others are introverted and sit back. We get set in our ways. Synagogue Board Development offers a series of stretching exercises to loosen up what can be talked about and what can be felt.

Synagogue Board Development is designed to stretch the team's muscles toward the transformational pole.

It is designed to stretch the team's muscles toward the transformational pole.

Maimonides taught that wisdom existed between the poles of two extremes. The wise person strove to find the point where he could be guided by both poles: "If a man finds that his nature tends or is disposed to one of the extremes, or if one has acquired and become habituated to it, he should turn back and improve, so as to walk in the way of good people, which is the right way. The right way is the mean in each group of dispositions common to humanity: namely the disposition that is equally distant from the two extremes in its class" (Moses Maimonadis, Mishne Torah, *Laws of Ethical Conduct* 2:3). Leaders need to have confidence, but they also need to be humble about what they don't know. Transformation does not mean that we are encouraging people to speak in tongues in ecstasy. Rather, we are asking that they learn to hold their tongues and listen to their teammates more intentionally. Leaders need to create a safe space to share concerns. In this space leaders bring attention to the needs of every individual while protecting the overall community's mission.

BOARD RESPONSIBILITIES

Board Source (a national association of non-profits) lists ten key responsibilities for the board. I will focus on three.

1. *Determine the organization's mission and purpose.* It is the board's responsibility to create and review a statement of mission and purpose that articulates the organization's goals, means, and primary constituents served.

Action: The board needs to develop a leadership plan.

2. *Recruit and select the leadership.* The board must reach consensus on the leader's responsibilities and job descriptions, then undertake a careful search to find the most qualified individual for the position.

Action: The synagogue must hire senior staff (rabbi, cantor, educator, executive director) and recruit lay leadership. I recommend that leaders develop shared goals and values and a process of mutual review for

key lay and professional staff leaders. If the lay community has no written values, goals, and objectives, the staff will find it difficult to implement these things. The nomination process needs to be collaborative and to reflect the congregation's values.

3. *Support the leadership and assess his or her performance.* The board should ensure that the paid and unpaid leadership has the moral and professional support he or she needs to further the goals of the organization.

Action: You need to find a method that works for your congregation. I recommend a mutual review process. The board and staff need an accountability plan to ensure that they are working on a common goal and all know their parts.

Using Different Leadership Approaches

Leadership expert John Kotter asserts that in times of change the leadership pole becomes relatively more important for organizations.

LEADERSHIP TOOLS

Part of the leadership development process is learning to manage your personal leadership style. Peter Senge of MIT in *The Fifth Discipline Field Book* has said that leaders need to be able to use different orientations depending on the situation they are encountering. Leaders need to use a variety of tools. If all you have is a hammer, everything looks

Synagogue Board Leadership Wheel of Learning

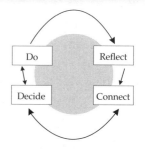

like a nail. There are times where they must *reflect, connect, decide,* and *do*—to everything there is a season.

Strategic Concepts Worksheet

A strategic plan will move from reflection about the environment, to the connection between mission and context, and ultimately to the decisions to be made around goals and actions—the *leadership plan.* As the team moves into implementation, they enter the world of action. They charter teams and create job descriptions—the *delegation plan.* They put plans to work. The cycle comes full circle as they review the impact of their work—the *accountability plan*—and enter a new round of reflection.

Strategic Steps

1. Review Mission Statement

The planning committee should review the current mission statement to see if it answers the following questions. If there is no mission statement, they need to create an interim statement for the SBD process using a framework inspired by Light. They will revisit this later in the planning process.

Model Mission Statement Framework

1. Summary: Helping members engage in meaningful Jewish worship, study, and community within the tradition of ＿＿＿ Judaism. We provide K–12 religious school, worship services, adult study, social programs, and lifecycle events.
2. Owners: Jewish members of all ages in the ＿＿＿ area

3. Customers: members, staff, and community partners
4. Outcome: Development of committed, knowledgeable, and caring Jews dedicated to the building of our Beit Midrash, Beit Tfillah, and Beit Knesset
5. Reputation: a community that is knowledgeable, warm, welcoming, caring, inclusive, and relevant to the lives of our members and dedicated to *tikun olam,* support of Israel, and *klal Yisrael.*

Mission Statement of Temple Sinai (Roslyn, New York)

The mission statement of Temple Sinai of Roslyn, New York, has many of the elements of a model mission statement framework. It also has the merit of moving beyond the tired cliches of the axiomatic statement and provides a real taste of their culture.

Temple Sinai is our sanctuary; a place to study, worship, and assemble. The essence of our synagogue has been to bring together diverse individuals to learn together and to pray together—to be unified as Jews. Our size and diversity have become resources that contribute to our strength. In order to create the caring and sharing temple family and Jewish community that Temple Sinai is, our professional and lay leadership have collectively recognized their responsibilities, both implicit and explicit, as educators and role models, to reach and teach our temple membership. We are always defining, refining, and redefining our short-term goals in light of our larger mission to meet the individual and collective religious, spiritual and emotional needs of the congregation.

Our obligation is to deepen the body of Jewish knowledge and religious commitment of our members of all ages by fostering the study of Jewish texts and tradition so as to help them make informed responsible choices in developing their Jewish identities. We also strive to provide support, loving-kindness, and concern to our congregants. In addition, we hope to enrich and increase participation in personal and communal worship and enhance and broaden the Jewish content of each member's daily life.

Supporting Statement (shows how new activities support core purpose)

This year Temple Sinai celebrates its fifty-fifth anniversary, yet the vision of its founders remains with us today. We continue to be a warm and caring Jewish community dedicated to perpetuating Judaism and meaningful Jewish expression. And at the same time, we are constantly exploring alternative modes of worship to enrich our spiritual and intellectual experiences. Throughout the years, young and old alike have entered the doors of our sanctuary to pray together, learn together, and share both happy and sad occasions with their temple family. Our collective social conscience mandates that we participate in the life of our people, our community, our country, Israel, and beyond. Here in Roslyn, we have created a Jewish community in the true sense of the word—it is our Jewish home away from home.

Exercise: Review the statements. Do you see examples of the five key elements? You might note these. Sinai added a supporting statement. What does this addition say about how their leadership works?

Exercise: Further explore and develop the theme of "warm and caring."

2. DEVELOP JEWISH VALUES STATEMENT— BEHAVIORAL COVENANT

Let's look at how a congregation might further describe their values and goals.

Example: Jewish Value *Hachnassat Orchim* (Welcoming)

We seek to welcome new leaders as Abraham did. In a dangerous desert environment, he risked opening up the flaps of his tent to include strangers at his table. He personally attended to their needs and offered them his best food and drink.

3. DEVELOP STRATEGIC PRIORITIES AND GOALS

Example: Outreach

Beth Israel will strive to become more welcoming to both longstanding members and new prospects. It will reach out to current and unaffiliated members and create policies and an annual calendar of events targeted to attract them. Board members will take the lead in these efforts.

4. DEVELOP SMART GOALS

Example: Planned Events

We will conduct four community Shabbat dinners, targeting the unaffiliated. We will focus on welcoming and will minimize formal membership recruitment techniques.

A SMART performance goal is an end that the paid and volunteer staff strives to reach; it directly supports the larger congregational vision. When individual staff members participate in writing their own performance goals, they have a clearer understanding of what is expected. Clear performance goals provide staff with purpose, clarity, and direction.

To be effective, performance goals must be specific, measurable, attainable, relevant, and time bound.

Specific
Goals must be easily understood. They must tell precisely what the employee will accomplish.

Measurable
Goals must be easily measured so that there is no question as to whether the staff is successful in reaching the goals.

Attainable
Goals must not be too difficult or too easy. If the goal is too challenging, the staff may become frustrated. A goal that is too easy won't prompt any changes in behavior.

Relevant
Staff goals must be congruent with the overall goals of the congregation.

Time bound
Goals must be bound by specific time parameters and deadlines for completion.

Exercise: Write an effective goal statement. Remember to keep it SMART!

Questions: Why are the goals on the left not SMART? Look at the example of a goal on welcoming. Now rewrite the other goals using the SMART approach.

A Starting Place	How Would You Make It Better?
Be more welcoming	Example: SMART Goal We will conduct [measurable] four [specific] community Shabbats dinners targeting the unaffiliated. We have done two over the years, so we feel this is realistic [attainable]. This goal is relevant [relevant] because we chose welcoming as the theme of our board retreat last August. We will focus on welcoming and will minimize formal membership recruitment techniques. We will focus on the total number of people who attend, the percentage that come to another event that year, and those who express an interest in joining.
Ensure that the office staff becomes more productive.	
Increase board involvement.	
Improve communications.	
Run board more like a business.	
Observe a higher standard of professionalism at meetings.	

5. Develop Action Plans

Once we have goals, we will need to encourage committees and task forces to develop action plans.

Example: Board Governance Committee Action Plan
Provide clear accountability for implementation.

Possible Actions	Who	When
Create an overall board governance committee.	EC-Saul	August 1
Create a 12-month agenda.	EC-BGC	October 1
Develop a calendar for key policy and strategic presentations from committee sponsors.	EC-BGC Chairs	November 1
Coordinate calendar with executive director.	President Bill-OG	
Develop internal and external communications plan.	PR-Barb	January 1

In the case above, the community had the values of being dedicated, effective, and future-focused, but when the leaders reviewed their focus, they were not doing very much in these areas. They had the language in their mission statement, but they had not really focused their energy on driving these values.

The values, goals, and actions exercise helped define how the board might do its part to be more welcoming. That is what strategy is about. When something is a priority for the organization, then its goals and actions need to be aligned to make it happen.

Assignment: First answer the following open-ended questions, then fill out the quantitative Synagogue Board Development Self-Assessment on page 24.

Synagogue Board Development Questions

What is working well on the board?

What could be improved?

What should be the number one priority for the board this year?

Why is this important to you?

What would you most like to contribute to the board this year?

How could the leadership help you in this effort?

Congregational Needs Assessment

Synagogue Board Development does not probe as deeply as a strategic planning process. The first SBD workshop does, however, deal with the Leadership Plan. The Leadership Plan looks at where we are going. It challenges us to clarify our goals for the year. At the end of Workshop One we hope to have some overall goals for our board (training, better meetings, job descriptions etc.) We may also have some goals we want to assign to some committees. In your applications you stated several congregational goals. We will review these as well as the results of this congregational needs assessment.

We designed this to be a simple survey because we wanted to have something that would be easy to do and get a high rate of return from board members. The consultant will summarize the data and identify some areas for future reflection and discussion.

Strategic Reflection

Synagogue Board Development seeks to encourage strategic thinking. Strategy has to do with allocating our resources (money, people, focus, meeting time, etc.) That is why we go beyond asking about performance and inquire about importance. A few minutes of your time on this assessment might provide more focus for your board team for the year.

When we look at the congregation's needs in terms of the organization's "performance" as well as their importance to the mission, we will find opportunities for action.

1. Areas we believe are important and where we are not performing as well as we would like. How can we create an action plan to address these?
2. Areas that are important and where we are performing well. How can we build on these—promote these strengths?

Synagogue Board Development Self-Assessment

Name:

Mark the box that best applies to your view.	(1)	(2)	(3)	(4)
Leadership	Strongly Agree	Agree	Disagree	Strongly Disagree
I am able to name the key issues facing our board for the upcoming year.				
I can name the overall goals the board wants to reach this year.				
Our meetings follow a detailed timed agenda sent out in advance.				
I have the congregational information that I need to make good decisions.				
Each year our board spends time getting to know one another and teambuilding.				
Our board is confident and optimistic about achieving our set goals.				

Delegation	Strongly Agree	Agree	Disagree	Strongly Disagree
I feel that my talents and interests are known and valued.				
Our board conversations are respectful and affirming of differing views.				
Each board committee reviews its purposes and direction at the start of the year.				
Each key committee makes at least one major presentation to the board yearly.				
We have a process to track whether board and committee objectives are met.				
The time I spend in board meetings is productive and worth my being there.				

Accountability	Strongly Agree	Agree	Disagree	Strongly Disagree
I am encouraged to examine my commitments to the board: financial, work, attendance, etc.				
Board meetings end with a check on the effectiveness of our work that day.				
Key committee chairs do a regular self-assessment of their board work.				
Board officers and the chairs they supervise have regular conversations.				
The board encourages mutual accountability of members to one another.				

What is the one thing I would most like to see our board work on? Why?

3

Workshop 2

Delegation Plan

Understanding the Synagogue Organizational Structure

Business leaders try to tap the talent and resources of their employees. Synagogues need to utilize their members' and staff members' gifts to help the organization but also to fulfill their spiritual mission. Synagogue work is *torah lishma*, spiritual work for its own sake.

Some nonprofit organizations are set up for the board to make policy. They expect the executive and professional staff to implement plans. Many assume that the synagogue can be run as a nonprofit. According to Board Source, this rigid model is unrealistic. "The old dictum that the board sets policy and the staff carries it out is oversimplified since many important organizational issues require a partnership" (Board Source Assessment 2002). Board members will need to provide hands-on expertise from time to time. The rabbi and other staff will have to provide leadership on policy formation.

Other congregations break from the nonprofit model and set up two professional areas. The rabbi is usually established as the head of the professional programmatic staff (some call this the chief religious officer), and the executive director reports to the board for administrative areas. This model is realistic about the need for specialization but creates a dual reporting process that can lead to conflicts over turf, and these tensions can in turn get in the way of a unified mission and teamwork (i.e. alignment).

Still other congregations have evolved into very flat organizations in which the lay leadership is expected to integrate the many elements of the congregation. In this model the rabbi may not be asked to supervise anyone. The rabbi functions as a spiritual leader, and the senior staff receive their contracts and primary supervision from officers of the board. This model puts pressure on the lay leadership to supervise individuals and to ensure collaboration, which can be pretty difficult in a voluntary leadership situation where leaders come and go. One thing seems clear: whatever model one chooses, there will be areas of potential confusion and conflict. Paid and volunteer staff must work on clarifying their roles, responsibilities, and authority. It is a rare congregation that does not need improvement in this area.

All of the models require teamwork and collaboration. There is too little coercive power and too few financial incentives to move the voluntary community without their "buy in." Collaboration is not just a tactic to get more volunteerism. It is a fundamental Jewish value. In Maimonides' ladder of *tzedakah*, one of the highest forms of doing justice is to help someone find a job. In synagogue leadership, this means to help each member find a way to bring his or her gifts to the building of the synagogue. Studies show most synagogues are not doing a very good job in this area. If they are going to do better, they need to experiment with a more collaborative management system.

Concentrated and Dispersed Authority

In business school we were taught rules about delegation. When I was in management (hospital and manufacturing), I learned that supervision is an art. Sometimes it made sense to empower people more. Other times I needed to give much more specific instruction and monitor performance more closely. Ken Blanchard's work on supervision, *Situational Leadership II,* is a great resource for learning how to adapt strategies based on the skills of the individual and their motivation.

Synagogue leaders need to understand the challenges of supervision, such as when to delegate and empower and when to hold fast to their authority. We can learn these lessons from the tradition.

Delegation. When Moses was trying to manage the Israelites in the desert, his father-in-law advised him to delegate some of his responsibilities. "The thing you are doing is not right; you will surely wear yourself out" (Exod. 18:17). He then challenged Moses to create a chain of command.

Empowerment. In another section Joshua challenged two men named Medad and Eldad who were feeling very empowered and spiritual. They had felt called and had begun to prophesy and act as prophets in the camp (Num. 11:26). This disturbed Joshua, son of Nun, Moses's attendant from his youth. He spoke up and said, "My lord, Moses, restrain them." Joshua had been working in the hierarchical system with Moses. Now he saw new people who felt they could be trusted to hear God's voice and describe God's plan. He didn't like it.

There is in Jewish history a grave concern about false prophets. We can understand Joshua wanting to maintain "concentrated authority." We will see long-standing leaders in strategic planning who become concerned as relatively new arrivals begin to vision, or "prophesy in the camp." Leadership creates a welcoming committee, but then new members begin to show up with lots of new ideas that aren't always welcome.

Moses tried to coach Joshua to be more open to new voices. Moses said to him, "Are you wrought up on my account? Would that all the Lord's people were prophets" (Num. 11:26–29). Moses understood, like a good workshop leader, that there are times when we need more energized participation—it's worth the risk.

Maintaining boundaries. While the tradition establishes the importance of delegation and empowerment, it also establishes the importance of concentrated authority. Leaders must maintain boundaries. In chapter 6 of *Kadima,* "Authority: Learning to Lead," we discuss types of authority. In my SVP planning process, the rabbi establishes one boundary and the board establishes the other. SVP is not a pure democracy, but it is collaborative, inclusive, and democratic.

Moses faced this in the challenge to his concentrated authority in the conflict with Korah. God helped him establish a boundary. The narrative of the desert wandering is full of chapters in which the people complain about the mission and the leadership. We see several people running on the "Let's go back to Egypt" platform! Korah made a direct challenge to Moses, asking, "Who appointed Moses to be over everyone?" "They combined against Moses and Aaron and said to them, 'You have gone too far! For all the community are holy, all of them, and the Lord is in their midst. Why then do you raise yourself above the Lord's congregation?'" (Num. 16:3).

While the tradition warns leaders not to lord it over the community, it also understands that some people understand God's mission better than others. We all can approach God, but the priests are better positioned, for prayer and purity are their daily practices. Moses was better positioned to lead than Korah. He had been with God face-to-face. Addressing God's mission had been his daily practice.

In this case, Moses's authority was well established. He was chosen by God (traditional authority) and had a relationship with God. He had provided extraordinary leadership (expert authority), had been selfless and sacrificing, and had been a consistent and strong leader (charismatic authority). In this story Moses's leadership was concentrated, but it was for a noble purpose—for the sake of Heaven. Korah and his followers were punished and laid low, for the survival of the Jewish people was on the line.

The concentrated authority of leaders will be most tested when the boards make a decision concerning a professional staff person. I noted earlier that less than 20 percent of the congregation does most of the work. A very small percentage of these core members are involved in personnel management. When there is a controversial decision about the rabbi or other staff, various members will suddenly become more engaged and ask, like Korah, "Why then do you raise yourself above the membership? Who empowered you?" I deal with this in my article in *Alban Weekly* called "When Bad Things Happen to Good Congregations." It is a fundamental principle of nonprofit governance that not all stakeholders are created equal. Some have stepped up to work on the board. They have an ethical and fiduciary responsibility to lead. They have sat through hours of meetings to earn the right to lead. While boards are ultimately responsible to their members, members can vote with their feet and leave, and they can vote with their ballots at annual meetings.

We talked about values and behavioral covenants in Workshop I. The organizational charts and the job descriptions for the EC, board, and committees have values embedded in them. We need to understand the descriptions of each model.

Authority

Concentrated . . . . Dispersed

Decisive leadership	Consult larger congregation
Consistency of leadership—continuity	Bring new people into leadership
Expertise, experience	Grassroots decision-making experiments
Tradition-established stakeholders	New stakeholders
Official leadership	Gifted leadership (Woods)
Maturity	Spontaneity

Excesses of Concentrated End of Scale

Small groups have the power to derail initiatives.
Leadership is recycled.
Leadership becomes burnt out (Yitro).
Power groups become entrenched (Case: 20 years, 10 couples).
In group–out group feelings.
Those in authority become insensitive to diverse groups, new members, changing environment.

Excesses of Dispersed End of Scale

People are confused about proper role of rabbi, staff, executive committee, board, and congregation (Case: the Fair Report).
Leadership turnover.
Strong leadership is distrusted (Case: Board without business-people).
Decision-making process is slow.
People pursue own agenda—advocacy.

ORGANIZATION CHARTS

Chief Executive Officer

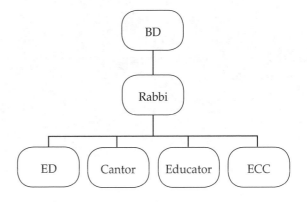

Advantage: One staff leader sets staff agenda and takes the lead in evaluating staff. They are charged by the board to implement mission, policy, and goals. This is the classic nonprofit model.

Disadvantage: Many rabbis don't want to be responsible for administrative operations. The role of rabbi has expanded. There is pressure to provide more spiritual leadership. Many rabbis don't have the skill set to supervise administrative issues.

Chief Religious Officer

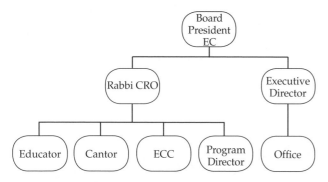

Advantage: The rabbi does not have to be burdened with administrative and financial issues; executive directors can be recruited to address these. They can report to board members with administrative backgrounds.

Disadvantage: Not all professional staff are evaluated by one unified staff supervisor. This can lead to communication problems and coordination between programmatic goals and financial policies.

CSL

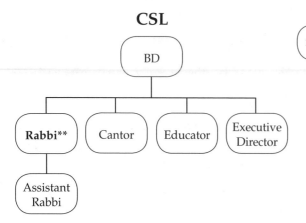

Advantages: The rabbi may not want to be a staff leader, may not have the skills or temperament for supervision, or may be a gifted pastoral care person or scholar. This model allows the rabbi to give up his line responsibilities. It tends to work best where the other staff are very skilled and experienced in their roles and need minimal supervision. They know how to work with the rabbi and one another. It helps if the board has a very highly disciplined management style and a strong personnel system.

Disadvantage: If the staff needs supervision, they do not have one professional to turn to. If there is turnover and new staff need to be mentored and oriented, there may be a vacuum. When there is a vacuum, lay leaders may fill it. Some may be ill equipped to do this.

Lay Leadership

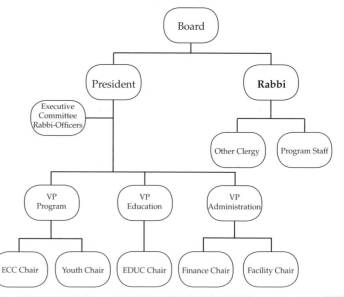

KEY LEADERSHIP CHALLENGES

- Clarify roles and responsibilities for all levels of governance (executive committee, board, committee) appropriate for your size.

- Work with staff to encourage them to provide overall goals and policies.
- Work with rabbi to encourage collaboration between staff areas.
- Ensure alignment of committees; you don't want them working at cross-purposes.
- Make assignments based on "situational analysis" of task and talents (Blanchard).
- Clarify reporting of lay and staff leaders.
- Get feedback on volunteer and lay staff performance.

ROLES AND RESPONSIBILITIES

How then should each level of governance be organized? Below are some of the key responsibilities leaders must undertake. The left column is from Board Source. It describes classic nonprofit governance approaches. In the right column are synagogue challenges. These lists should provide a starting point for further discussion. I try to group key responsibilities into the three plans. Given the differences in size, culture, and context that we have discussed, there is no "one size fits all" model that we can offer here.

Board Responsibilities (Board Source)	Synagogue Leadership Challenges
Determine the organization's **mission and purpose**. It is the board's responsibility to create and review a statement of mission and purpose that articulates the organization's goals, means, and primary constituents served.	Leadership Plan: Understand how that mission is grounded in sacred traditional texts and traditions. Board members make a commitment to grow in their understanding of their mission, the congregation's mission, and God's mission.

Board Responsibilities (Board Source)	Synagogue Leadership Challenges
Select the chief executive. Boards must reach consensus on the chief executive's responsibilities and undertake a careful search to find the most qualified individual for the position.	Delegation Plan: Recruit paid and unpaid staff to drive congregational ministries. Develop job descriptions for key staff that spell out essential functions and core competencies. Recruit senior clergy and administrative staff to lead their teams. Determine the role of unpaid staff in key ministries. What are the tasks? What are transformational purposes?
Support the chief executive and assess his or her performance. The board should ensure that the chief executive has the moral and professional support he or she needs to further the goals of the organization.	Delegation Plan: Develop a sacred partnership with professional staff inspired by the idea of a covenantal relationship rather than a solely contractual relationship (see attached). Develop mutual ministry goals and a mutual review process. Accountability Plan: Develop a performance management system. Recognize that the paid staff will normally have a more formal set of goals and more formal review.
Recruit and orient new board members and assess board performance. All boards have a responsibility to articulate prerequisites for candidates, orient new members, and periodically and comprehensively evaluate their own performance.	Leadership Plan: Motivate others to join the mission. Develop a nonminating committee process to recruit and orient new members. Develop a process to increase teamwork, goal setting, and feedback for the board and individual members. Delegation Plan: Develop a job description for the board members. Establish both essential functions and core competencies.
Provide proper financial and operational oversight. The board must assist in developing the annual budget and ensuring that proper financial controls are in place.	Leadership Plan: Determine what to measure and monitor. Make sure that the budget reflects the priorities and purpose of the organization.

Board Responsibilities (Board Source)	Synagogue Leadership Challenges
Ensure adequate resources. One of the board's foremost responsibilities is to provide adequate resources for the organization to fulfill its mission.	Leadership Plan: Educate the community about the financial situation and budget priorities. Role model financial stewardship though a personal commitment to raise money and contribute personally.
Ensure legal and ethical integrity and maintain accountability. The board is ultimately responsible for ensuring adherence to legal standards and ethical norms.	Leadership Plan: Model high ethical standards. Encourage transparency in processes, relationships, and decisions.
Enhance the organization's public standing. The board should clearly articulate the organization's mission, accomplishments, and goals to the public and garner support from the community.	Leadership Plan: Communicate the mission, values, and visions to staff, stakeholders, members, and the community. The religious mission calls us to "teach it to our children," so it is not enough just to do our synagogue task; we need to communicate our purposes and our work.
Determine, monitor, and strengthen the organization's programs and services. The board's responsibility is to determine which programs are consistent with the organization's mission and to monitor their effectiveness.	Accountability Plan: Prune old programs (Drucker) and explore new programs to meet the needs of changing community. Encourage staff and members to share responsibility for new programs development, recruitment and implementations (synagogue engagement groups, parlor meetings, etc.).

Responsibilities of the Individual Board Member (Develop Behavioral Covenants)

Responsibilities of the Individual Member Common Board Core Competencies	Excercise: If these competencies were present, what would you see?
Listening: Listen, analyze, think clearly and creatively, and work well with people individually and in a group.	

Responsibilities of the Individual Member Common Board Core Competencies	Excercise: If these competencies were present, what would you see?
Openness: Possess sensitivity to and tolerance of differing views; a friendly, responsive, and patient approach; and community-building skills.	
Curiosity: Welcome new people and ideas. Take time to brainstorm and vision. Support experiments.	
Transparency: Be open about motives and goals. Be forthcoming about issues and the way decisions will be made.	
Personal integrity: Strive to be what you say you are. Resist temptation to cut corners; have a developed sense of values and concern for your nonprofit's development.	
Be prepared: Prepare for and attend board and committee meetings, ask questions, take responsibility, and follow through on a given assignment.	
Tenacity and energy—don't give up.	
Generosity: Contribute personal and financial resources in a generous way according to circumstances.	
Positive public voice: Open doors in the community. Promote the gift of synagogue membership. Focus on strengths and opportunities.	
Welcome: Be inclusive and open to diverse membership.	
Compassion and empathy: Reach out to learn about others. Approach the SBD reflective process as a way to understand self and others.	
Passion for programs: Help strengthen a program area of the organization. Look for new ideas.	
Fairness and consistency	

Responsibilities of the Individual Member Common Board Core Competencies	Excercise: If these competencies were present, what would you see?
Joy—have fun, smile	
Humility	
Confidentiality: Do not disclose privileged board conversations outside of the board.	
Commitment to develop others—servant leadership: Teach it to your children and mentees. Cultivate and recruit board members and other volunteers.	
Yirat ha Shem, fear of God, and commitment to sacred partnerships: The value that helps shape all of the above is the commitment to developing *brit kodesh*—sacred relationships.	

Assignment: Now that we can visualize our core competencies, how might we write them down as expectations? What does our tradition say about these behaviors and values?

Board Members' Agreements (Operating Covenants)

Individual Board Member Responsibilities: Essential Functions	Board Covenants to Explore
Attend all board and committee meetings and functions, such as special events.	Attendance Policy
Be informed about the organization's mission, services, policies, and programs.	Define Expectations for Training: review briefing book; attend orientation if new.

Individual Board Member Responsibilities: Essential Functions	Board Covenants to Explore
Role model core values of organization.	Agree to engage in dialogue about plans to increase commitment to the following: • home practice • participation • learning • worship • leadership • financial contribution • welcoming (positive attitude)
Review agenda and supporting materials prior to board and committee meetings.	Participate in meetings. Honor participation of others (no one speaks twice until everyone has had a chance to speak once).
Serve on committees or task forces and offer to take on special assignments.	Members should commit to be assigned to a committee. Discourage individuals from editorializing at board meetings if not carrying their share of committee work.
Inform others about the organization.	The board speaks with one voice. Support the majority decision. Speak in a positive way about the congregation and its leadership.
Suggest possible nominees to the board who can make significant contributions to the work of the board and the organization.	Agree to make suggestions and solicit prospects for board.
Keep current on developments in the organization's field.	Be aware of developments. Be active in attending events so that you know what is going on. Meet expectations regarding annual meeting, board training, *bimah* honors, etc.
Follow conflict of interest and confidentiality policies.	Don't disclose board's business or debates.
Refrain from making special requests of the staff.	Honor lay-staff boundaries. Clarify roles.
Assist the board in carrying out its fiduciary responsibilities, such as reviewing the organization's annual financial statements.	Be knowledgeable about financial issues.

Exercise: Propose three helpful board covenants.

1.

2.

3.

Now make a composite list of all of the suggested covenants. The leadership team will then develop a draft for the board to consider.

Responsibilities of the Leadership: President and the Executive Committee

Officers: Essential Functions	Synagogue Observations
Provide a sounding board for the president and the rabbi.	As the EC listens to the special needs of both clergy and lay leadership, they are better able to understand how to manage the tensions between these roles.
Develop overall strategies and set overall 12-month agenda for the board.	Most boards are caught up in the day-to-day management and problem solving of the board. If boards are going to work to learn new things and experience more transformational relationships, these experiences must be built into the board's calendar (*Stepping Forward*, chapter 2, "Developing Leadership Gifts").
Explore new ideas suggested by committees and individuals. Vet proposals and help prepare them for the board.	Leaders practice a form of servant leadership. They evaluate how well the EC has helped committees be more effective.
Handle crisis issues that cannot wait until the next regularly scheduled board meeting.	If the roof is leaking above the sanctuary, we need to stop the leak short term. We can then address long-term capital issues in a planned process.
Other Functions	
Function as personnel committee in smaller congregations that don't have a separate human resources or personnel function. (In congregations over 500, I recommend a separate committee.)	If you don't move the personnel tasks to a separate personnel committee, it can eat up all of the EC planning time.
Develop a coaching and oversight process for key committees. Help them identify and develop programs, policies, and recommendations.	Synagogue volunteers are voluntary and loosely coupled. They come and go. They often have a narrow focus of synagogue life. Officers help provide a holistic view of the synagogue and leadership through their oversight function. This also helps provide continuity.
Create an ombudsman process (not just president) to help the president channel member feedback to the right people.	Helps reduce pressure on president.

Exercise: Write down your thoughts and feelings about the executive committee job description.

GOVERNANCE STRATEGIES

To address these responsibilities, leaders must develop some governance strategies.

1. *Define "ends," or outcomes.* Provide volunteer and professional staff the overall goals. Help clarify overall expectations and ensure that they get feedback when projects are completed. Work to give them room to implement the plan in their own way. Nonprofit expert Carver writes, "Having board policies in place ahead of time allows board and staff alike to know whether a paid or

unpaid staff proposal is approvable, since all the criteria by which approval is given are clear for everyone to see." Implement the "stacking containers" concept. Don't invest so much energy in solving the problems around an incident (small container). Step back and try to establish the policy framework (big container) first. This will make all future decisions easier and make delegation possible (Blanchard).

2. *Empower paid and unpaid staff to develop "means."* Committees should be empowered to find the "means" to address issues to work within a framework of policy. The executive committee and board should work to create the overall policy before they are tempted to micromanage the means that the committee has chosen.

3. *Set realistic SMART goals.* Today's synagogue volunteers have limited time. Committee members and other volunteers may withdraw if they don't clearly understand the role and function of the committee and its connection to the larger leadership structure and to the mission of the synagogue (alignment). If a goal is too low, there is no urgency to start. If the goal is too high, it discourages action.

4. *Define how decisions will be made.* The role of the executive committee, board, and committees should be reviewed every year. Leaders should develop an A-B-C process for decisions. C issues should be delegated to the committees and the staff within general guidelines. Resist the following:

- Becoming entangled in trivia to avoid feeling like rubber stamps. Don't nitpick.
- Acting as a "committee of the whole"
- Debating low-level issues (C decisions)
- Seeking approval from the congregation on "C" issues.

5. *Define role of staff and/or clergy leader.* Some nonprofit theorists feel that in today's nonprofit environment, the staff leader needs to provide the leadership to help the board perform its leadership and policy role.

Some church consultants feel that the clergy leader needs to go beyond providing vision and policy. The clergy leader has to help reshape the board experience so that it is more transformational and spiritual—to change the nature of the work that leaders do.

Start Doing!
Annual Plan

- Prepare a twelve-month agenda that creates a narrative for the year. It should outline key topics for each season (membership in August, budget in February, and new board member orientation in late May, etc.). It is easier for a traditional board to accept innovations that are spread out over a 12-month period.
- Take time for team building each year. Design group conversations that ensure that people feel welcomed. Ensure that they get to know something about the Jewish journeys of fellow leaders and are given the chance to share their story. Use team-building tools (MBTI, CSI, LSI, etc.) to reframe relationships. Write job descriptions for the most important board jobs (offices, key chairs).
- By focusing on key topics, you can reframe the board meeting. Connect *dvar* to topics, creating rituals around them. Invite a committee person to share some personal reflections about these issues, and use narrative notes to describe them.
- Create a record of board deliberations (personnel issues, however, are

an exception).

- Have committees prepare a committee charter. Define the roles of staff and volunteers on the committee. Are some committees open to all? Do others require background experience or orientation (religious school)? Do some require a level of commitment (ritual, i.e., attend services)?
- What are the committee tasks the staff is charged to do (e.g., keep membership records)? What things are the unpaid staff charged to do (e.g., greet new members at dinners)?
- Define what policies need to be addressed during this twelve-month period. Give the assignments to committees, professional staff, and their executive committee liaison. Keep policies in a binder in alphabetical order by topic.
- Remember, bylaws are meant to serve your mission. If some are barriers, develop a plan to address them.
- Review the basics of your meeting process. While Robert's Rules of Order can be cumbersome for most synagogues due to their excessive formality, some elements are very helpful. Use elements that help define board etiquette and process board *derech eretz* (manners). Incorporate them into a list of board behavioral covenants. Examples:

    — Ensure that "all voices are heard." The role of president or meeting chair is as meeting facilitator, not as primary advocate for a position.
    — The board should "speak with one voice" or not at all. Debate within the board, but don't criticize decisions to community (Sanhedrin)

    — When members make suggestions in the middle of a discussion, you can place these on a piece of newsprint with the header "Parking Lot." This allows the board to honor suggestions and come back to them under new business without losing focus on the agenda.

- Develop a communications plan to inform the congregation about the key issues for the year. Use multiple channels of communication—sermons, bulletins, handouts, announcements, posters, etc. Consider a town meeting to get input on key issues of the twelve-month agenda.

Start Doing!
Monthly Meeting

The executive committee or officers should design the agenda for the upcoming meeting at least one week in advance. This is one of their most important responsibilities.

The rabbi should suggest a ritual or a text to start the meeting. Experiment with this in several meetings during the next six months. The theme might be worked into the beginning, middle, and end (the power of three). Look at S3K examples of rituals (www.synagogue3000.org). This learning should ideally tie to key themes of the annual plan. This is part of executive committee agenda planning.

- Have key critical facts (vital signs) on a one- to two-page sheet (revenue, expense, membership, etc.). This models a commitment to learning and literacy.
- Continuously explain the board's structure and priorities. Explain what the executive committee, offi-

cers, committee, and board are doing on a current issue. This models a commitment to transparency.

- Define what committee reports should be on the agenda. Committee reports should primarily be sent by mail. Committees should present only when a major issue is to be reviewed.

- Consider distributing the old minutes and all committee reports as a consent agenda. This goes to each member. Unless the EC hears of a problem, these documents are automatically approved at the start of the meeting.

- Create a timed agenda that helps clarify which topics deserve more time. The timed agenda also ensures that the group won't run out of energy for items later in the agenda. This models a commitment to leadership.

- Start by reviewing action items from the last meetings. Review the SMART goals checklist, which lists the status of top initiatives. Manage by exception. This models a commitment to accountability.

- Do a two-minute process check at the end of each meeting. See what worked well and what could have been done better. This models humility and openness.

End with a closing ritual—a personal reflection, a text, etc.

Reports to: VP Membership

Committee Responsibility Summary
(Bylaws, Executive committee charge)

Meetings—Monthly

Essential Functions

Recruit new members. Make them aware, welcome them, follow up with them, facilitate their joining, integrate them.

Retain current members. Gather data on the following: What gives meaning to members? Why do they join (member profile)? Why do they leave (exit interview)? Create a process to find a home for those seeking one (affinity groups—new mothers, singles, book clubs, hiking and biking enthusiasts, business networkers, short-term *havurahs*). Encourage self-reflection of board and staff. How are our programs working? Develop a process to evaluate programs (prune old and test new).

Create an integrated communications plan. Develop a process of educating the executive committee, the board, and the congregation about what you are learning. Develop a message (compelling versus cliches) that talks about what you are passionate about and excel at. Create vision language that gives members, staff, and prospects a compelling picture of your community. Create an integrated marketing and communications plan (brochures, bulletins, sermons, website, posters, handouts, signage, ads that reinforce these themes).

Develop volunteers. If there is no separate volunteer coordinator or committee, develop a volunteer management system to recruit, assign, train, and recognize volunteers.

Core Competencies
(Qualities of Team)

Core competencies: openness, curiosity, flexibility, innovation, transparency, etc.

Key skills sought: marketing, public relations, desktop publishing, social work, writing. How might you find them?

MODEL TIMED AGENDA
(7:00-9:00 P.M.)

Call to Order

Dvar Torah (5–10 minutes)

Consent Agenda
Minutes, committee reports (reviewed if not approved)

Clergy and Program Staff Report (5–10 minutes)
Rabbi's report—key initiatives update, important values staff is supporting

Administration (5–10 minutes)
Executive director or administrator's report—key operational issues
Treasurer's report—key financial metrics, important budget variances to discuss, cash management

President's Report (5–10 minutes)
Review key goals for year
Review agenda

Agenda Topics (50 minutes)
Old business—includes parking lot from last meeting
New business—on agenda (A and B decisions)
Provide change to new work groups

Committee Reports (20 minutes)
Priority topics chosen by leadership (EC, officers)
Designed for group participation and discussion
Designed to expand learning of board (include committee charter)

Good and Welfare (5 minutes)

Process Check (2–5 minutes)
How did we do? What worked well? What could be improved?

Close

(Time: 97–117 minutes)

A Helpful Proposal

In order to make the board more affective, leaders need to encourage better proposals. Effective proposals explain their rationale. They are transparent about purpose. They have SMART goals that the board can monitor. Let's look at a helpful proposal.

Committee: Fund-Raising

I. Background on Issue (What do we need to know before exploring the recommendation?)

The congregation has a $50,000 deficit. It is a new congregation with little history of significant fund-raising. The focus in the past has been the capital campaign for the current building. There is little depth in solicitors. The membership is not accustomed to being asked for major gifts. Fund-raising and endowment make up less than 5 percent of the revenues in the budget. Based on conversations with denominational leaders, this is below average for comparable congregations of our size.

II. Project or Policy Purpose (How does it contribute to the committee's overall purpose?)

Our values statement calls for us to be financially responsible in maintaining the synagogue. It also calls for us to inspire others to increase their commitment to all synagogue activities. Moreover, we have the goal of finding multiple ways to engage our membership. The LRP committee felt there was a need for more social events.

III. Project Description

The fund-raising committee would like to create a casino night with a raffle as a new fund-raiser. The members on the committee are _____, etc.

IV. Policy Issues

Are there any legal restrictions on this type of gambling?
    What concerns do the rabbi or others have in terms of Jewish law and values?

V. Organizational Issues

Is the date clear?
    Will any other part of the organization have a conflict with this plan?
    What other committees could collaborate on this?

VI. Specific Objectives

List at least three measurable objectives:

1. Create a large steering committee of 10+ people
2. Sell 250 raffle tickets at $100 each. Solicit prizes (condos, products, services).
3. Solicit 10 sponsors—one for each game table (10 x $500).
4. Attract 200 members. Charge $50 per person to include buffet. Have cash bar.
5. Target contribution to operating budget: $25,000

VII. Actions Required

List the major roles required for project development and implementation, e.g., scheduling, publicity, preparing worksheets, contacting vendors, etc. For each element, estimate the amount of time required for implementation.

Action	Time Required	Responsible	When
Recruit steering committee	10 hours—will take 60 days after approval	Judy Stern	December 1, XXXX
Set up catering	10 hours	Executive Director	May 1, XXXX

List any special skills, talents, or interests that may be required: game hosts; raffle ticket salespeople; in-kind gifts solicitors; party planners; food service people; decorators; public relations.

VIII. Other Projects Considered
Art auction; gala dinner; ad book; honor a member.

Exercise: Take one upcoming committee proposal and use this format.

4

WORKSHOP 3

ACCOUNTABILITY PLAN

Why is accountability so important? We need to be accountable to ourselves and the community and ultimately to God. The Jewish practice of *tzedakah* encourages every Jew to help improve the world—to make it more just. *Tzedakah* is a developmental value. Expectations were low for a person who had been living in a town for only a few months. But the longer that person was a "citizen," the more of the community's obligations he was expected to share. "One who settles in a community for thirty days becomes obligated to contribute to charity together with other members of the community. One who settles for nine months becomes obligated to contribute to the burial fund of burying the communal poor" (Zevit).

As leaders, every day we are expected to become more engaged in our communities. The Torah says that we must not hide ourselves from people's needs. We are challenged to stop our journey to help someone who is in distress. Even when we see an adversary on the road, we are to treat him with the respect we have for all human beings. We must get out of our cart and help him raise his ass and his cart if they are off the road. The Midrash argues that by doing this work we will have a change in attitude. Leaders are meant to be connected.

Congregational leaders understand that many peripheral members have been "living in towns" for a long time without fully accepting their share of their community's concerns. They may not be fully committed to doing their share to support weekly wor-

ship or logging volunteer hours. They may not have paid their share of the capital fund. If we just lecture to them about the gap between their practice and the community's needs, many will turn a deaf ear. We need to find a way to help them make the connection between the needs of their families and the needs of the broader community.

ACCOUNTABILITY VERSUS ENTITLEMENT

Americans have been empowered to advocate for their interests. As Michael Hammer writes in *The Agenda*, we live in a culture where "the customer is king." In such a culture, advocating for one's individual consumer rights is considered a desirable skill. Companies are constantly under pressure to create the "new and improved." It is not surprising that Jewish communal observers have noted that the congregants often bring this consumer attitude to their approach to synagogue membership. They want a "new and improved shul" now.

Our biblical narrative of the Israelites in the desert lists a series of complaints. The masses complained, "We were better off in Egypt," Korah complained about Moses's leadership, and the spies who investigated the Promised Land complained about God's plan.

LEADERS INCREASE ENGAGEMENT

- *Communal focus.* Judaism is realistic about human nature. People will complain. Jewish tradition challenges these individual consumers to give up some of their individual rights for the sake of the community's well-being. The synagogue cannot create a special sacred community if everyone pursues his or her own self-interest to the max.

- *Partnership practices.* Synagogues must manage the needs of consumers, but they depend on leadership from members. In a volunteer organization with hundreds of members and only a few staff, how can the mission succeed if people are standing with their hands in their pockets waiting to be served?

- *From complaint to contribution.* When leaders are held accountable for their part of the solution, they often transfer their energy from complaining to providing. When you are accountable for your committee or task force, you also gain some humility for how hard it is to get things done in a volunteer community. Accountability reinforces a commitment to performance.

ACCOUNTABILITY TO SELF: PERSONAL COMMITMENT PLANNER

Rabbis have the responsibility to motivate their members to embrace their religious responsibilities. They challenge leaders to bring both spiritual gifts (the ability to move people to greater religious engagement) and personal skills and talents (the ability to get things done). If accountability is so important, then how do we get leaders to be more accountable?

Exercise: All leaders should fill out the following template. They will then share reflections on their experiences with one other leader.

Judaism starts with a value of focus on home practice. As we strengthen our practice,

we bring our values to the synagogue, the general community, and the world. In our SBD exercises we start with a reflection by the individual and then move to group agreements.

Personal Commitment Map Category	What I Am Doing Now	One Thing I Could Do in the Next 12 Months
Tfillah: observance/ worship; commitment to holiness; spirituality		
Talmud Torah: commitment to study		
Tzedakah: financial commitment		
Shalom Bayit: peace at home; practice with family		
Hachnassat Orchim: welcoming; outreach to new members and in-reach to current members		
Avodah: commitment to serve (doing committee work; supporting synagogue activities)		
Tikkun: social action (reaching out to others)		

ACCOUNTABILITY TO THE COMMUNITY: TAKING HOLD OF RESPONSIBILITIES

The board is empowered to work with the rabbi to lead the congregational organization. The board depends on its members taking key assignments. The handoff from the board to committee chairpersons is one way we ritualize our accountability to each other. The delegation plan sets the foundation for good accountability. It ensures that assignments are clearly stated and firmly grasped by the committee. Just as Joshua asks the people to recovenant after they cross the Jordan, so synagogue leaders challenge committees and teams to recovenant—to take hold of their responsibilities.

COMMITMENT TO OUR TEAM

The following questions were inspired by the work of the Union for Reform Judaism and the United Synagogues of Conservative Judaism on mutual review.

Chairperson's Self-Assessment

What goals did you set for the year?

What resources did you identify and request?

What difficulties or barriers did you face?

How could your leaders have provided more support?

What are three of your accomplishments that stand out in your mind?

What are some of the skills, talents, or areas of knowledge that you demonstrated?

What is the most important thing you learned this year?

How have you grown Jewishly through these experiences?

Questions

- What was it like to do the assessment?
- What was it like to share your review with a board officer?
- How could the officer help make this a more productive exchange?

I encourage the EC to monitor the key board goals (12-month agenda) and committee goals. They should take time to celebrate the completion of a goal just as students do when they finish a section of Talmud. We do not berate those with incomplete work. We coach them privately. We do praise publically those who were accountable.

Commitment to Track Our Goals *Byachad*

Initiative	Responsible Person/ Group	Jan	Feb	Mar	April	May	June
Report on exit interviews	Membership—Tom			X			
Write a welcoming plan	Membership—Tom				X		
Develop a new brochure	Communications—Barb					X	
Create a dues special offer	Finance and dues—Sam				X		
Offer a new open house—RS	Education—Jean		X				
Develop plans for youth room	Youth house—Irv, Janet						X

Commitment to Evaluate Programs

Leaders need to prune old programs and develop new ones. In an accountability culture, the members are encouraged to step forward and help develop new program ideas.

SYNAGOGUE ENGAGEMENT MODEL

In the synagogue engagement model, leaders brainstorm some viable ideas and then post them in the foyer and on the Web. They offer to be a resource to groups that want either to join or to lead a program. Leaders listen to the congregation but insist that these programs need to be a partnership. The synagogue engagement model helps leaders and members model accountability. Programs emerge when members step forward.

Commitment to Honor Behavioral Covenants

In previous workshops I encouraged you to think about board behavioral and operating covenants. Behavioral covenants address the expectations for individual board members, such as attendance, committee work, and financial commitment. We addressed some of these in the commitment exercise above. They also relate to basic manners, or *derech eretz*. Little things like committing to an RSVP for an event or a meeting or responding to a call or e-mail promptly can make a huge difference in a leadership culture.

ACCOUNTABILITY: GIVING FEEDBACK TO BOARD LEADERS AND CHAIRPERSONS

The leadership plan process helped us get more focused. The delegation plan process helped us clarify roles and responsibilities. Leaders, as I have argued, are expected to monitor the goals of these plans and have important conversations with the board and committee chairpersons. Yet, in my experience, the dominant situation in synagogues is a tendency for avoidance. Leaders are afraid to confront others because they are not sure how to engage them. They are also concerned about alienating the volunteers they have worked so hard to recruit. We want leaders to engage others but not in frustration and anger. "When a man becomes angry—if he is a sage, his wisdom departs from him, if he is a prophet, his prophecy departs from him. . . . When a man becomes angry, even if his greatness has been decreed for him by Heaven, he is reduced from his greatness" (*Pesah.* 66b).

How do we avoid the language of frustration? Just as we have rituals to help us plan a sacred community, so too we *plan* for healthy conversations. Since feedback is critical for healthy congregational relationships, in this unit we will explore how to engage in helpful feedback. We will consider the "covenantal caring conversation" (CCC) that goes beyond the language of business (contractual relationships) and stretches to develop more covenantal relationships.

The Importance of Feedback

Good feedback helps people to reflect on their performance throughout the year so that they are in a process of continuous reflection and improvement. It is essential for both paid and unpaid staff. The Johari Window (see below) describes this process of disclosure.

	Known to Self	Not Known to Self
Known to Others	Public area	Blind spots
Not Known to Others	Avoided, hidden	Unknown (nonrational)

Engaged leaders encourage others to let them know what is on their minds (disclosure) so that they can give them helpful feedback about what they are hearing and seeing. The CCC seeks to move more issues into the public area (be transparent) where things are known by us and other leaders. There are some blind spots I can't see without your help. There are some concerns and motivations that we can't discern unless another leader discloses them. Leaders need to learn to hold themselves accountable to manage difficult conversations and to learn new skills in giving effective feedback in a synagogue setting.

The more we understand what paid and unpaid staff are looking for in a work relationship, the more skilled we will be in motivating them. A Gallup study, *First, Break All the Rules*, found the following were questions that were most important to staff.

> ONCE WE LOOK AT WHAT STAFF MEMBERS SEEK, WE BEGIN TO UNDERSTAND THE IMPORTANCE OF GOOD FEEDBACK.

1. Do I know what is expected of me at work? (Role clarity)
2. Do I have the materials and equipment I need to do my work right? (Support)
3. At work, do I have the opportunity to do what I do best every day? Can I build on my strengths? (Empowerment)
4. In the last seven days, have I received recognition or praise for doing good work? (Positive attitude)
5. Does my supervisor or someone else at work seem to care about me as a person? (Covenantal relationship)
6. Is there someone at work who encourages my development? (Mentor relationship)[1]

The Performance Management Process

The following principles of performance management apply to both paid and unpaid staff in principle. Needless to say, they will be applied with more formality to paid staff. Feedback should be designed to address both the staff's needs and the organization's needs. Performance management eliminates the performance appraisal or annual review and evaluation as the focus and concentrates instead on the entire spectrum of performance improvement, development, training, 360-degree feedback, and informal performance feedback. Performance management moves from summative (looking backward) review to formative (looking forward) coaching. A performance management system includes the following elements:

1. Define the purpose of the job, job duties, and responsibilities.
2. Define performance standards for key components of the job.
3. Use SMART goals to define performance goals.
4. Hold interim discussions and provide feedback about employee performance, preferably weekly, summarized and discussed, at least, quarterly. (Provide positive and constructive feedback.)
5. Maintain a record of performance through critical incident reports. (Jot notes about contributions or problems throughout the quarter in an employee file.)
6. Provide the opportunity for broader

annual feedback. Use a performance feedback system that incorporates feedback from the employee's peers, customers, and people who may report to him.

7. Develop and administer a coaching and improvement plan if the employee is not meeting expectations.

8. Take necessary steps of improvement if the performance gap is not closed.

Performance Management Seeks to Avoid Common Feedback Pitfalls

In approaching feedback and evaluation, there are several principles that can be helpful. According to Edward Schein (*Process Consulting*, 1988), evaluation and assessment are helpful in identifying the skills in the organization and in providing feedback to improve performance.

PERFORMANCE MANAGEMENT MOVES FROM SUMMATIVE (LOOKING BACKWARD) REVIEW TO FORMATIVE (LOOKING FORWARD) COACHING.

Avoid these pitfalls:

- Failure to agree on goals.
- Vagueness and generality of message.
- Lack of transparency about feedback givers' motives.
- Withholding negative critical feedback to avoid conflict. This often occurs with long-term rabbinates.
- Procrastination. Should be relatively close (within a few weeks) to key event; if delayed, memory fades.
- Failure to find a receptive period (*teshuvah* literature). Don't criticize the rabbi after he or she delivers the HH sermon.

- Overreliance on negative feedback. Focus on reinforcement of the positive. (Blanchard, *The One-Minute Manager*, Buckingham Gallup).

Question: Why is performance management important for us?

The Performance Management Process Helps Balance Employment Relationships versus Covenantal Relationships

Most of us are familiar with the evaluation and feedback process from the corporate world. Although business benchmarks are helpful, synagogues are also governed by covenantal models. Susan Beaumont has developed a model at Alban that helps us compare the two approaches (see table below). The business model seeks to have a contractual relationship with associates based on utility—the maximum benefit to all—while the covenantal model seeks to develop mutual commitments and relationships. Building healthy relationships is one of the outcomes of the synagogue's mission. Once we understand this, we can see how synagogue feedback can strive to be somewhat "above the letter of the law." I am not suggesting, nor is tradition demanding, that we ignore poor performance. The tradition asks us to give feedback in the least negative way so we can maintain the relationship.

Element	Covenantal Relationships	Employment Relationships
Nature of the psychological contract:	Benevolence (The entity with greater power looks out for the interests of those with lesser power.)	Utilitarian (Collectively, we pursue a course of action that produces the greatest "pleasure over pain" for the greatest number of people.)
Focus:	Mutual need, mutual promise, mutual relationship	Supply and demand, maximize bottom line, outcomes
Values:	Submission, protecting the "least of these," the pursuit of justice, righteousness, and mercy	Offer acceptance, fairness, equity
Objective of the relationship:	Fulfillment of a promise	Fulfillment of a contract
Outcomes sought:	Restored community, right relationship, a blessed future	Career satisfaction, monetary reward, professional growth, job security
Staff members are:	Ministry participants, pastoral care recipients	Resources to be employed
Accountability requires:	Clearly stating expectations, honoring the covenant, reconciliation when the covenant is broken	Clearly stating expectations, honoring the conditions of the contract, mediation when the contract is broken
What failure looks like:	Isolation—broken relationship	Unemployment—terminated relationship

Susan Beaumont, "Stepping Up Supervision," Alban Institute, 2006.

Leaders need to manage the tension between a focus on contractual and covenantal relationships. Given what we have learned about what is most important to staff, it is good business to manage these perspectives. To create a mission-driven congregation, it is essential Jewish leadership!

From Avoidance to Engagement

When I work with congregational leadership, I sometimes become a lighting rod for their anxiety. I may be verbally attacked. My efforts may be minimized. I am a big man and am not easily minimized, and I have been in many conflict situations and thus am not easily frightened. I expect to meet resistance and therefore am not easily surprised. Nevertheless, I have experienced painful encounters. They hurt. If congregational conversations have caused me, as thick skinned as I am, so much pain, how do dedicated Jewish professional workers feel? Many of them were called to synagogue service to teach children, to lead us in prayer, or to pastor the troubled and ill. Many professionals I see are not ready for the culture of criticism. They begin to avoid issues.

I see leaders restrict congregational access to important information for fear of conflict. Sometimes an executive committee will ask the rabbi to step down without consulting the board. In other cases a major cost overrun is reviewed by the building committee but not fully explained to the congregation until much later. The results of a major worship study are not brought to town meetings. In all these cases, leaders start out on an important synagogue journey but don't finish their work. They try to avoid getting angry feedback from the community because they want to avoid getting hurt. When

COVENANTAL RELATIONSHIPS TAKE MORE TIME AND EFFORT, BUT THEY LAY THE FOUNDATION FOR STRONGER TEAMS.

all the information finally does come out, there may be a lot of pent-up frustration in the congregation. These conversations may not be so compassionate. When our leaders "cut corners" in their relationships with others, there are consequences. (Note that Jacob's deception of Esau lead to Jacobs's deception by Leah.)

In my experience, the dominant condition in synagogues tends to be *avoidance*. Leaders are afraid to confront others because they aren't sure how to. They are also concerned about alienating the volunteer staff they have worked so hard to recruit. Often their frustration bubbles up in anger with volunteers. It may erupt during contract negotiations with professional staff. We are to avoid angry encounters (we value self-control). To reduce the risk of such explosions, we need to find a way to engage in the right conversations at the right time. This is a conversation in private that protects the dignity of the other while being true to your needs and those of the community. Sometimes a conflict becomes so public that a community conversation is required. Healthy congregational conversations help keep conflict manageable.

LEADERS NEED A CONGREGATIONAL LANGUAGE THAT IS WORTHY OF THEIR MISSION, ONE THAT DEVELOPS COVENANTAL CARING.

ENGAGING IN DIFFICULT CONVERSATIONS

Feedback is a vital part of effective management and fulfills our value of planning. "What is the good way. . . ? To foresee consequences" (*Avot* 2:13). Leaders are challenged to give feedback when they feel someone is going in the wrong direction so they can ensure they do not damage themselves, others, or the community's mission. Planning requires feedback. "You shall surely rebuke your neighbor, and incur no guilt because of him" (Lev. 19:18). One way that leaders can reduce avoidance and procrastination is to plan to hold these difficult conversations.

The CCC, like other board behavioral covenants (see appendix), is based on core Jewish values. The CCC is more than a feeling of love or affection. It is rooted in the fundamental honor and respect that we owe another human being by virtue of God's creative power. God made man in his image (*b'tzelem elohim*), so we are bound by our covenant with God to honor our fellow human beings.

If one believes that the other person is in the image of God, it is easier to imagine that he or she has needs to serve the community that go beyond money, benefits, and career aspirations. It also suggests that he or she has needs for a relationship that is not just based on such business factors as supply and demand, return on investment, or short-terms goal achievements. The value of *b'tzelem elohim* suggests that one of our organizational goals is to develop special sacred relationships. How do we do this? We do it by carrying key Jewish values with us to these difficult conversations.

Humility. "I am but dust and ashes," says Abraham (Genesis 18:27). When we are humble, we are much less likely to move carelessly without getting input from others. Humility makes us slower to judgment.

Respect for all. "Let the honor of your fellow human being be as precious to you as your own: (*Avot* 2:15). When we respect someone, we see that person in full. We pay attention. Everyone has strengths and weaknesses. Everyone, according to the tradition, has his or her day. When we respect others, we tend to render a more balanced view of them.

Good manners. "Without good manners there is no Torah" (*Avot* 3:21). Good manners (*derech eretz*) help reduce the focus on our personal agenda and individual needs. If I am constantly thinking about the needs of others, I am less likely to do something insensitive. Good manners build a foundation for trust.

Self-respect. Since we are made in the image of God, we deserve respect. "And God created the human being in his own image" (*b'tzelem elohim*). While we are challenged to "put ourselves in other shoes," we are not asked to ignore our own legitimate needs, feelings, and wants. We have the right to stand up for ourselves.

Self-control. "Who is mighty? He who conquers his passion" (*Avot* 4:1). Many of our values require judgment. They are not black and white. Learning to control our emotions—particularly anger—helps us make better decisions. One tool that helps facilitate covenantal caring conversations is Nonviolent Communication, developed by Dr. Marshall Rosenberg. I highly encourage leaders to explore this framework. Covenantal caring is not servitude. Rabbi Hillel's famous words speak of the need to find a balance between your needs and the needs of others: "If I am not for myself, who will be for me; if I am only for myself, what am I?" (*Avot* 1:14).

How do we encourage accountability without adding to the culture of criticism that we find in so many congregations? How do we give helpful feedback without alienating the volunteers that we are working so hard to recruit? How do we give feedback to dedicated staff that work long hours to help us build our community? How do we

avoid such unhealthy practices as blaming, generalizing, and labeling?

It is not enough to know Jewish values. We also need the "how to" to put them into practice during our board year. I suggest leaders start at the top and learn to give helpful feedback. We can make our concerns known but in a less judgmental way. Leaders can let others know the following:

Observations
The concrete behaviors they are observing that impact them and their community.

Feelings
How they feel in relationship to what they are observing.

Needs
The needs, values, and desires that are creating these feelings for them.

Requests
The concrete actions they request in order to enrich their lives and their communities.

Story: Sue's Wednesday Hot Call List

Sue is on the welcoming task force. She has been an active and energetic member. Now the congregation has entered the implementation stage, and Sue is eager to get things going. Sue is a very capable volunteer who has helped out on various successful events over the years. On two or three occasions this year she seemed to leave some tasks incomplete until very close to the event and then showed great anxiety about those tasks. On Wednesday she came into the office and asked the temple administrative assistant, Barbara, to make her issues an immediate priority. She saw that reservations for the dinner were a little light, and she wanted a major effort to call the general membership. This was not the practice for the Friday Shabbat dinner project, but Sue felt very motivated since this dinner was one of the action items of her welcoming task force.

It was also difficult to manage on Wednesday with Friday less than two days away. Sue didn't know that one of the office staff was scheduled to leave for half of Thursday. The office would be short-handed. She did not work through the executive director, Frank. Sue calls the president to complain. What could the president do? The following is a model conversation using nonaggressive language—a covenantal caring conversation. It does not ignore the issue, but it speaks to the volunteer in a way that may be more likely to be heard.

Observations. "I appreciate your committment to Beth El. I understand that you came to Barb at 10:00 a.m. on Wednesday to help work on set-up plans for this Friday. I was told that Barb was doing a priority assignment for Frank."

Feelings. "I appreciate all of the projects here at Beth El, but I get concerned when members ask our office staff to do things without coordinating with Frank. I feel it confuses the staff and frustrates me."

Needs. "I have been encouraging Frank to improve communications and planning with the whole staff. I have also asked him to clarify office processes with the lay leadership. As you know, we have been working under tough budget constraints. We did not agree to Frank's request for another part-time worker. We have asked the staff to learn to work more effectively with the resources they have. The executive committee has felt the need to be very careful with staff resources. Your desire to call one hundred members on Wednesday and Thursday for a Friday dinner would have to move ahead of current priorities we have set."

Request. "I would like you to know how much we appreciate your commitment to these Friday dinners. I hope you can appreciate our needs for planning and prioritization.

"We will see if we have time to make a few calls. Do you have a list of fifteen to twenty members you think might be prime prospects? These could be people who usually come but have not yet responded.

"I would like to hear how you feel about the concerns I just raised. I am always looking for ways to create better communications, planning, and teamwork."

REFLECTION ON A COVENENTAL CARING CONVERSATION

The president appreciates Sue's energy. He also appreciates all of the work Sue has gone through to motivate volunteer efforts. The president is probably frustrated, but his words are not full of anger. He does not shame Sue by generalizing—"You have no concerns for the needs of staff." Rather, he focuses on the the specific behavior she is concerned about. "A person who publicly humiliates his fellow man has no place in the world to come" (*Avot* 3:14).

The president starts by sharing his appreciation. The problem is that he is frustrated and has needs and values that are not being met in this case. He does not suggest that she is incompetent or ill-willed, but her behavior is creating an issue for him.

He is not callous. "Do not harden your heart and shut your hand against your kinsman" (Deut. 15:7). Even though the responsibilities of being president are sometimes challenging, he brings a great deal of empathy and energy to this conversation. He respects her. She matters to him (covenantally), and he wants the conversation to be a caring one.

The process of nonviolent communication starts with an observation about the behavior. We are not asked to ignore a problem. We start by simply trying to pay attention to what is going on. First, we discipline ourselves to describe our observations; next we are challenged to share our feelings. We hold ourselves accountable to let the other person know what we are feeling when we bring our feelings into the "public realm" (Johari).

Needs. Next, he speaks on behalf of the leadership and the community. He is not focusing on his personal style preferences. Perhaps Sue is more extroverted than he likes. He is not addressing her from a personal agenda—although he may not like the Friday night format. He is speaking for the "sake of Heaven," for the higher community purpose of an effective and cooperative congregation.

Requests. Now the president asks for Sue to work with him. Up until now he simply asked for her to listen. Now he proposes some ideas he would like her to consider. He does not ask her to admit she is wrong.

Exercise: Take one case in which you needed to give someone feedback. How could you do this using the covenantal caring conversation approach?

IMPLEMENTATION: THE BOARD DEVELOPMENT PLAN

SBD is a beginning. Leaders must work with these ideas and integrate them into their leadership culture. Over the next six months, leaders should work to address the following needs:

KEY SBD FOLLOW-UP WORK.

Ensure effective SBD agenda.
Encourage committee charters.

Encourage at least one "helpful proposal." (pp. 38–39)
Have EC develop and track SMART goals.
Review feedback from board meeting (process checks).
Review implementation of behavioral and operating covenants.
Develop a 12-month board agenda
Communicate progress to the congregation.

IMPLEMENTATION: LEADERSHIP

As leaders move forward to change the board culture, they will experience resistance. Synagogue Board Development changes need the support and guidance of some dedicated people. Who should take on this responsibility?

SBD is a process of adaptive change. It provides some key leadership exercises and encourages the development of new team practices. We started the first workshop by asking all of the board to cross their arms. We then asked them to cross them the other way. Everyone sensed the awkwardness. We have preferred ways of doing some things. We have muscle memory.

1. *Executive committee.* The executive committee is a natural group to implement and guide SBD changes. As we discussed in workshop 2—the delegation plan—the key responsibility of the executive committee is to help the leaders plan the work of the board. The risk of the executive committee "owning" SBD is that it will not get adequate focus among all of the other issues of the executive committee.

2. *Select group of officers and others.* An alternative is to assign SBD to a few champions who will speak to SBD issues at the board and do SBD planning. This might include the SBD project chairpersons, some

board members, and some executive committee officers.

3. *Governance committee.* One idea that is growing in nonprofit literature is the idea of a governance or trustees' committee. This committee takes a role in developing the human resources of the board. It coordinates the efforts of the following kinds of committees:

- Nominations
- Leadership development
- Board training

This *Byachad* workbook would be helpful for nominating committees. They could review the job description and behavioral covenants with prospects. They could promote effectiveness of the board and its committment to improvement. *Byachad* means working hard to get input from the rabbi and current officers about prospective board members.

COMMUNICATIONS PLAN

The leadership should write an article about what they learned from SBD and some of the changes they are implementing.

Exercise: Write a congregational update on SBD and the board development plan.

TOWN MEETING—ANNUAL MEETING

Review the results of the needs assessment (appendix A). Pick five goals that are the most important. Welcome attendees to go to the goal they would most like to discuss. These would be facilitated by board leaders. Make a list of breakout group participants. Record their ideas. Set up a follow-up meeting to discuss the next steps.

Exercise: Develop an agenda for a congregational town meeting.

MENTORING SUPPORT

Consider developing a relationship with a mentor. It could be a past president or a leader from another SBD congregation. The mentor would work with the leadership on implementing the SBD plan.

We have a cultural memory. The board table is full of traditions, and these don't change overnight. Social scientists call these paradigms or mental models. We have frameworks for seeing things and ordering our realities. SBD wants us to look at how we set our leadership seder table from a different perspective.

Exercise: Invite an outsider to sit in on one of your board meetings and provide feedback on your board process.

CONCLUSION

Synagogue Board Development asks leaders to reflect, connect, decide, and do. For everything there is a board season. The 12-month agenda helps leaders place key issues throughout the year.

I hope you continue to use the tools of the SBD to strengthen your agreements, policies, and processes. As you learn to work *Byachad* you will come to understand your Jewish mission. You will understand what God is calling us to do in this place.

Appendix A

Congregational Needs Assessment

Instructions

- Review the congregational needs list. Adapt to meet your congregation's situation.
- Rate how well you are addressing the issues: 1=Very Well, 2=Well, 3=Passing, 4=Poorly, 5=Very Poorly.
- Add up the score and provide an average score for each need (i.e., Define a mission=2.5).
- Blow up the chart and do the following priority-setting exercise: everyone has four stickers and uses them to vote for the needs they feel are most important now.

At the end of the exercise, leaders will know how the team feels about how well they are addressing key needs and which needs are most important now.

Congregational Needs		
We need to . . .	How well are we doing? 1=Very Well, 5=Very Poorly	Comments
Leadership Development		
Define roles and responsibilities of officers and board		
Assess board member satisfaction		
Set clear goals and objectives		
Define a mission		
Define roles and responsibilities of nominating committee		
Worship		
Strengthen our ritual committee		
Examine new forms of worship		
Explore creative venues for worship		
Explore musical options		
Operations—Human Resources		
Strengthen our house committee		
Help office staff be more responsive to membership		
Clarify lay staff roles and responsibilities		
Strengthen computer-office systems		
Personnel		
Develop respectful communications between lay and staff		

We need to . . .	How well are we doing? 1=Very Well, 5=Very Poorly	Comments
Develop healthy communications between lay leaders		
Learn how to manage conflict and make decisions		
Membership		
Attract new members		
Engage current members		
Understand our members' interests and wants		
Understand membership satisfaction		
Identify and utilize members' talents		
Finance		
Develop a better dues structure		
Develop creative ideas for fund-raising events		
Develop an endowment		
Develop designated gifts		
Youth Programs		
Increase participation		
Train staff and volunteers to work with youth		
Connect with regional and international youth programs		
Adult Education		
Encourage knowledge of Jewish texts, thought, and practice		
Encourage knowledge of Hebrew and synagogue skills		
Israel		
Motivate members to go to Israel		
Connect members to Israeli insitutions		
Programs		
Develop more singles programming		
Develop more seniors programming		
Develop more family programming		
Develop more outreach to intermarried couples		
Develop more small-group programming (*havurot*)		
Develop more social action programs		
Develop more "Caring Community" programs		
Facility		
Improve sanctuary		
Improve school		
Improve social hall		
Improve office		
Improve parking and grounds		

Appendix B

Membership Profile

Personal

Name: _____ Gender: M F Date of Birth: _____

Address:_____
Street   City   State   Zip

Phone: (____)_____ Fax: (____)_____

E-mail: _____ Cell Phone: (____)_____

Marital Status: Single Married Separated Divorced Widow(er)

Ages of Children:_____

Employer:_____ Occupation: _____

Work Phone: (____)_____ Fax: (____)_____

Work E-mail: _____

College Major _____ Graduate School Major _____

Growing up, with which branch of Judaism was your family affiliated?

Orthodox Conservative Reform Reconstructionist Non-affiliated Other:_____

What have been some of the most important stepping stones in developing your Jewish identity and practices?

Synagogue Life: Committee Interests

For each of the following committees, please check the box that reflects your interest level. Also, indicate if you are a former/current chairperson or member of the committee. (Each committee is described on the back of this form.)

Committee Interests	Very Interested	Somewhat Interested	Not Interested	Committee Interests	Very Interested	Somewhat Interested	Not Interested
Adult education				Marketing/public relations			
Men's club				Membership			
Building				Parent association—religious school			
Cemetery				PTO—preschool			
Chesed (caring)				Programming			
College outreach				Ritual			
Endowment				School committee			
Finance				Sisterhood			
Hazak (seniors)				Young professionals			
Honorials/memorials				Youth commission			
Long-range planning				Other:			

Explore your number-one interest. Why is this so important to you?

Skills/Interests

For each of the following areas, please check the box that reflects your interest level.

Skill/Interest	Very Interested	Somewhat Interested	Not Interested	Skill/Interest	Very Interested	Somewhat Interested	Not Interested
Art				Sports (specify)			
Clerical				Education/teaching			
Computer				Torah reading			
Crafts				Drama			
Creative writing				Israel			
Finance				Holocaust			

Skill/Interest	Very Interested	Somewhat Interested	Not Interested	Skill/Interest	Very Interested	Somewhat Interested	Not Interested
Grant/proposal writing				History			
Health services				Hebrew			
Hospitality				Yiddish			
Humor				Bible			
Library				Rabbinics			
Music				*Tefillah/davening*			
Photography				Other:			

If you could work on one area of synagogue life, what would it be?

What skills, interests, and assets could you bring to this work?

Appendix C

Board Improvement Ideas—Possible Operating Covenants

Board Improvement Ideas—Operating Covenants	Resp.	Date
Develop committee charters for most important committees.		
Plan committee reports.		
Officers get a list of key policy issues to review for year.		
Use board proposal template for most important proposals.		
Do "check in" on important issues.		
Plan retreat in August.		
Plan annual meeting. Engage members about goals.		
Provide board orientation book.		
Review job descriptions of executive committee, board, and committees.		
Post descriptions on the Web and update annually.		
Post mission statement on the Web. Share key approaches to address mission.		
Dvar torah or ritual to start.		
Attend 75 percent of meetings. Can't miss three in a row.		
Term limits—three two-year terms as a general board member.		
Term limits—two two-year terms as a committee chair.		
Start on time.		
End in two hours or negotiate additional time.		
Review action items from last meeting after minutes approved.		
Pass out goal-tracking form.		
Prepare written agenda one week in advance.		
All committee reports in writing.		
Rabbi's and administrators' reports in writing.		
Do a process check at the end of the meeting.		

Appendix D

Clarifying Commitments: Committee Worksheet

I. Define Team

Membership Committee   Date

Chair

Members

Board or SC Liaison

Key Committees to Coordinate With

II. Define Purpose/Goal: Charge from SC/Board

III. Vision

If your task force was extremely effective in improving your area of congregational life, what would the congregation look like in five years? Pretend that you are a reporter who is observing the community five years from now. What are teens doing? What is the board doing? What are people learning? How are they worshiping? Provide a sketch for your area of focus (leadership, worship, etc.).Write this up in a bullet list. If you want to present this in a creative way, great.

IV. Strategies/Direction

Note key values and ideas that have emerged from the process. Review values statements and dominant themes. The SC may choose to provide additional direction to groups.

V. Performance Goals and Objectives/Schedule

What do we need to address our strategic goal? List most important objectives. Use extra page if necessary.

Objective should be:

Specific. Describe what team is to accomplish.
Measurable. A goal should be measurable so that one can determine if it is successful.
Attainable. A goal must be challenging but achievable.
Relevant. Performance objectives need to be consistent with the overall values and strategic goals of the synagogue.
Time bound. Goals should have deadlines for completion.

VI. Schedule

Note time frame requested by board.
Group objectives into three categories:

- Short term—within six months
- Medium term—within six to twenty-four months
- Long term—two years plus

Appendix E

For Further Reading

Andringa, Robert C., and Theodore Wilhelm Engstrom. *Nonprofit Board Answer Book: Practical Guidelines for Board Members and Chief Executives.* Washington, DC: BoardSource, 2001. This is a practical guide to classic nonprofit management issues. The organization also has a helpful Web site at www.boardsource.org.

Aron, Isa. *Becoming a Congregation of Learners.* Woodstock, VT: Jewish Lights, 2000. Dr. Aron is the leader of the Experiment in Congregational Education (ECE) initiative at HUC's Rhea Hirsch School in Los Angeles. This is an excellent book on the change processes. She provides organizational ideas, team-building exercises, and training ideas. It is a very practical book.

———. *The Self-Renewing Congregation.* Woodstock, VT: Jewish Lights, 2002. This book follows up on the Experiment in Congregational Education approach and addresses other elements of synagogue leadership and community.

Barna, George. *The Power of Team Leadership.* Colorado Springs: WaterBrook, 2001.

Blackwell, Roger D. *From Mind to Market.* New York: HarperCollins, 1997. Blackwell is a consumer trends consultant to companies such as The Limited. He looks at the socioeconomic and demographic changes (discontinuities) impacting American culture and suggests marketing and customer-relations strategies.

Bookman, Terry, and Bill Kahn: *This House We Build: Lessons for Healthy Synagogues and the People Who Dwell There.* Herndon, VA: Alban Institute: 2006.

Bradford, Robert W., and Peter J. Duncan. *Simplified Strategic Planning.* Worchester, MA: Chandler House Press, 2000. Offers a simplified version of corporate strategic planning for small business. The authors offer the book as part of their seminar and consulting practice.

Bridges, William. *Managing Transitions.* New York: HarperCollins (Perseus), 1991. Provides a model for facilitating groups to accept the loss of old structures and to celebrate new opportunities.

Brinckerhoff, Peter C. *Faith-Based Management.* New York: John Wiley & Sons, 1999.

Carver, John. *Boards That Make a Difference.* San Francisco: Jossey-Bass, 1997. Carver is one of the leading experts on nonprofit governance. He consults for major boards such as the American Cancer Society. He argues that boards must focus on making policy and insuring the mission of the organization. They should avoid micromanagement of staff work.

Clawson, James G. and Marcia L. Connor, eds. *Creating a Learning Culture: Strategy, Technology, and Practice.* Cambridge: Cambridge University Press, 2004.

Cohen, Gary S. *Welcoming New Members.* New York: Synagogue, 2000.

Collins, Jim. *Good to Great and the Social Sectors.* New York: HarperCollins, 2005.

Covey, Stephen R. *The Seven Habits of Highly Effective People.* New York: Simon & Schuster, 1989.

Dyer, William G. *Team Building.* New York: Addison Wesley, 1995. Good basic overview of the elements of team building. Provides training exercises and questionnaires to assist in assessment.

Drucker, Peter. *Managing the Nonprofit Organization.* New York: HarperBusiness, 1992.

Eisen, Arnold M., and Steven M. Cohen, *The Jew Within: Self, Family and Community in America.* Bloomington: Indiana University Press, 2000. This important book looks at various sociological studies on Jewish beliefs and practices. It also combines the in-depth interview process that Wade Clark Roof, Bruce Greer, and Mary Johnson have used in *A Generation of Seekers: The Spiritual Journeys of the Baby Boom Generation.* These interviews yield a portrait of the peripheral or marginal Jew. Eisen suggests that these Jews represent 60 percent of the Jewish community. Understanding their attitudes is critical in terms of developing strategies to engage them.

Gaede, Beth Ann, ed. *Size Transitions in Congregations.* Herndon, VA: Alban Institute, 2001. Size transition has been a core competency of Alban. Gaede revisits Rothauge's pioneering work on the implications of growth and change.

Gladwell, Malcolm. *The Tipping Point.* Boston: Little Brown, 2000. This is a brilliant and innovative review of the sociology of fads and epidemics. It considers how certain opinion makers can start a trend and how certain messages can resonate more than others. It also looks at the role of context in determining if a trend will take hold.

Goleman, Daniel. *Emotional Intelligence: Why It Can Matter More Than IQ.* New York: Bantam, 1995.

———, Annie McKie, and Richard Boyartis. *Primal Leadership: Realizing the Power of Emotional Intelligence.* Boston: Harvard Business School Publication, 2002.

Hammer, Michael. *The Agenda.* New York: Crown Business, 2001. Hammer is the developer of business process reengineering and other innovative management approaches. He has written a very accessible overview of the critical management and leadership skills necessary to compete in the twenty-first century.

Hardaway, C. Kirk. "FACTs on Growth." Hartford: Hartford Institute for Religious Research, 2006. http://fact.hartsem.edu/CongGrowth.pdf.

Heen, Sheila, Bruce Patton, and Douglas Stone. *Difficult Conversations.* New York: Penguin Putnam, 1999. This book builds on the research of the Harvard Negotiation Project. It develops a model for managing "difficult conversations" involving issues of conflict, performance appraisal, conflicts in values, and interpersonal relations. It is essential training for anyone in congregational leadership.

Heifetz, Ronald. *Leadership Without Easy Answers.* Cambridge, MA: Harvard University Press, 1999. A brilliant and innovative view of the role of leadership. Heifetz looks into the factors that promote serious adaptive change. He is head of the Leadership Education Project at the JFK School at Harvard. This is a must read for those considering synagogue transformation.

Heller, Zachary, ed. *Re-envisioning the Synagogue.* Hollis, NH: Hollis, 2005.

Herring, Hayim, and Barry Schrage. "Jewish Networking: Linking People, Institutions, and Community." Boston: Wilstein Institute of Jewish Policy Studies, 2001.

Hudson, Jill. *Evaluating Ministry.* Herndon, VA: Alban Institute, 2002. Excellent basic introduction to issues surrounding clergy and lay leadership feedback and evaluation.

———. *When Better Isn't Enough.* Herndon, VA: Alban Institute, 2005. Reviews the challenges of clergy leadership in a post-modern environment.

Katzenbach, Jon R., and Douglas K. Smith. *The Wisdom of Teams.* Boston: Harvard Business School Press, 1993. This is a basic text for modern business organizational process. It explains why teams that are properly designed, led, and rewarded can make a difference. Katzenbach is one of the most experienced consultants at McKinsey & Company.

Kotter, John P. *John P. Kotter on What Leaders Really Do.* Cambridge, MA: Harvard Business Review, 1999. Kotter is a major consultant to Fortune 500 companies and Matushita Chair of Leadership at Harvard. He focuses on the need for leadership during times of change and identifies critical skills that leaders need.

Kouzes, James, and Barry Posner. *The Leadership Challenge.* San Francisco: Jossey-Bass, 2002. An exhaustive overview of research and theory of leadership issues.

Leventhal, Robert. *Kadima: Stepping Forward.* Herndon, VA: Alban Institute, 2007.

———. "Re-imaging the Rabbi Lay Leadership Partnership." *Congregations,* Summer 2004.

———. "The Role of the Executive Committee," *Congregations,* Summer 2006.

———. "The Synagogue Leadership Agenda," *Congregations,* Spring 2005.

———. "Teamwork in the Synagogue."

United Synagogue Review, Spring 2003.

———. "When Bad Things Happen to Good Congregations," *Alban Weekly,* 2005.

Light, Mark. *The Strategic Board.* New York: Wiley, 2001.

Mann, Alice. *Can Our Church Live?* Herndon, VA: Alban Institute, 1999. Mann explores options for congregations that are in trouble.

Oswald, Roy. *The Inviting Church.* Herndon, VA: Alban Institute, 1987. Looks at research on how new members make decisions. Also examines the stages in the incorporating process: inviting, greeting, following up, orienting, incorporating, joining, and sending people to recruit others.

———, and Robert E. Friedrich. *Discerning Your Congregation's Future.* Herndon, VA: Alban Institute, 1996. This book provides an approach that has become popular with Protestant churches. It was originally developed to identify factors that created vitality relative to inviting new members. It offers some excellent models for creating community conversations and for facilitating whole-system learning events.

Pava, Moses. *Business Ethics.* New York: KTAV, 1997.

Parsons, George D. and Speed B. Leas. *Understanding Your Congregation As a System.* Herndon, VA: Alban Institute, 1993.

Rendle, Gilbert R. *Behavioral Covenants.* Herndon, VA: Alban Institute, 1999. Rendle looks at factors that create conflict in congregations. He proposes methods to improve congregational conversations and develop helpful agreements.

———. *Leading Change in Congregations.* Herndon, VA: Alban Institute, 1998. Rendle looks at the forces impacting congregations and the stages of the change process.

———, and Susan Beaumont. *When Moses Meets Aaron: Staffing and Supervision in Large Congregations*. Herndon, VA: Alban Institute, 2007.

———, and Alice Mann. *Holy Conversations*. Herndon, VA: Alban Institute, 2004. Reviews key strategic planning concepts for congregations. Provides many helpful exercises to encourage reflective conversations.

The Role of the Rabbi in the Congregation. Wyncote, PA: Reconstructionist Commission, 2001.

Roof, Wade Clark. *Spiritual Marketplace*. Princeton, NJ: Princeton University Press, 1999. Roof looks at trends among the baby-boomer generation who are now forty-five to fifty-five years old. He argues that boomers are seeking spirituality and a respite from their hectic lifestyles, but they are skeptical about organized religion and guard their right to "pick and choose" their beliefs and practices.

Rosenburg, Marshall B. *Nonviolent Communication*. Encinitas, CA: PuddleDancer, 2003.

Sales, Amy L. "The Congregations of Westchester." Waltham, MA: Brandeis, 2004. http://cmjs.org/files/FinalReport_Westchester_0304.pdf.

Schein, Edgar. *Process Consulting*. New York: Addison-Wesley, 1988. A basic text on the key elements of engaging systems as a change agent.

Sellon, Mary K., and Daniel P. Smith. *Practicing Right Relationship*. Herndon, VA: Alban, 2005. Provides a model for thinking about the behavior of leaders and exercises to help leaders manage their behavior and gain more personal mastery. Use with behavioral covenants.

Senge, Peter. *The Fifth Discipline*. New York: Doubleday-Currency, 1990. I believe in the five disciplines. They lay the foundation for looking at visioning processes. *The Fifth Discipline Field Book* provides many helpful cases and tactics.

Shevitz, Susan. "Organizational Theory." In *A Congregation of Learners*, ed. Isa Aron, Sarah Lee, and Seymour Rossel. New York, UAHC Press, YEAR. Shevitz looks at the characteristics of synagogue organizations and how they might impact educational initiatives. She suggests strategies to manage the environment.

United Jewish Communities. *National Jewish Population Study 2001*. New York: United Jewish Communities, 2003.

Weisbord, Marvin, and Sandra Janoff. *Future Search*. San Francisco: Berett Koehler, 1995. Provides a model for workshops for developing shared learning about organizational environments and produces vision, goals, and action plans.

Werthheimer, Jack. *Jews in the Center*. New Brunswick, NJ: Rutgers University Press, 2000.

Wind, Jim, and Gilbert Rendle. "The Leadership Situation Facing American Congregations: An Alban Institute Special Report," in *Leadership in Congregations*, Richard Bass, ed. Herndon, VA: Alban Institute, 2007. Looks at the overall crisis in clergy leadership.

Wolfson, Ron. *The Spirituality Of Welcoming: How to Transform Your Congregation into a Sacred Community*. Woodstock, VT: Jewish Lights Publishing, 2006.

Woods, C. Jeff. *Congregational Megatrends*. Herndon, VA: Alban Institute, 1996.

UAHC Task Force on the Unaffiliated. *The Life Cycle of Synagogue Membership*. New York: UAHC Press, 1991.

Appendix F

The 12-Month Calendar: Making Time for Leadership Work

Leadership Strategies

Review the Alban Board Self-Assessment (see pages 21–22). The strategies referenced in the left column below are from chapter 2, "Developing Leadership Gifts," of my book *Kadima: Stepping Forward*.

Leadership Strategies Developing Leadership Gifts	Board Experiments
Synagogue leaders use the symbolic frame to make the connection between current issues and traditional Jewish values.	Develop a theme for the year. Develop behavioral covenants. Do a process check on board behavior. Do self-assessments. Do personal commitment planner exercise. Change the shape of the room (lessons from teaching seventh grade). Meet in Sukkah.
Leaders need to seek out sacred spaces and find the sacred in new places.	Take a break for Minha/Maariv. Use several texts throughout the meeting—go beyond the three-minute dvar. Share a Jewish journey that ties to the issue at hand. Celebrate different gifts (Willow Creek—auto mechanics). Sing. Tie to holiday; meet in Sukkah; do havdallah and discussion group. Do a retreat with a hike and a picnic. Take time to acknowledge the sacred in seemingly secular tasks (checking in on a sick member, developing a chesed project, showcasing a volunteer gift). Provide a special blessing for the whole committee when they present.
Leaders can develop shared facts and work "to get on the same page."	Create congregational briefing book. Review important books on Jewish community. Debrief parlor meetings. Debrief visit to other congregations, conferences, etc.
Leaders reflect! When they better understand the needs they bring, they can better understand the needs of others stepping forward.	Do board retreat and set up Jewish journey discussions. Create active listening diads exercises. Use MBTI to study personality preferences. Develop process for reviewing a membership profile.
While leadership faces challenges today, a focus on the future can motivate and energize the leadership community.	Review overarching goals. Refer back to vision statements. Develop a values statement. Develop a 12-month calendar. Create 12- to 36-month goals.

Leadership Strategies Developing Leadership Gifts	Board Experiments
Give yourself a hand! Consultants, trainers, mentors, facilitators, and volunteer coordinators can connect to emerging leaders.	Find a facilitator for an annual retreat. Assign some mentors for emerging leaders. Use the officers to coach committee chairs. Create a small governance committee to review the work of the board; do process checks.
Synagogue change requires a big team to ensure a critical mass of players for action.	Do a joint session with the EC, the leadership development committee, the membership committee, and/or the volunteer development committee. Identify shared strategies for engagement. Recruit a leadership development class of existing and prospective leaders. Create some large stakeholder workshops.
Leadership development chairs are matchmakers! They provide a disciplined approach to recruit leaders, connect them to the right jobs, and ensure they are led effectively.	Find out what members are "very interested" in doing; see if you can develop a mission around this (Rick Warren). Use the annual board retreat to see where the whole board has energy (open space). Use parlor meetings to find out who can step forward to partner with the board on committees and projects. Develop synagogue engagement groups; find leaders first, then missions. Create a networking meeting to identify new leaders. Develop interviews—"It's just lunch!"
Leaders learn by doing. They want hands-on experience with projects for which they feel passion and with the partners they choose.	If they have passion, test it. Create experiments each year. Empower them to take some risks. Allow major committees (whole team) to come in and talk about their work.

Group Work: List three things I can bring back to our synagogue leadership.

1.
2.
3.

Exercise: Identify three things we might try in our meetings.

1.
2.
3.

Build a composite list. These will then be put into a draft of possible board improvements.

Appendix G

Kadima: Stepping Forward
Table of Contents (Suggested Reading)

NOTES

INTRODUCTION

1. James G. Clawson and Marcia L. Conner, eds., *Creating a Learning Culture: Strategy, Technology, and Practice.* (Cambridge: Cambridge University Press, 2004), 1–16.

CHAPTER 4

1. Marcus Buckingham and Curt Coffman, *First, Break All the Rules : What the World's Greatest Managers Do Differently* (New York: Simon & Schuster, 1999), 27–28.